"Rebecca Schumejda's *Hope is a Prison* is a gut-wrenching collection of poems shining an interrogation room light on the intersecting narratives connecting multiple victims of abuse. The familiar threads of poverty, family denial, shame, and failure of social safeguards are told in mostly short pieces that have been crafted with sharp detail, delivering the kind of visceral punch that stays with you for days after reading. These poems are best read in sequence like a short story. Stark black and white photographs, by Jason Baldinger further emphasize the cold rooms and environments where the events unfold. Rebecca Schumejda's voice is steeped in the immense humanity and experience of what she writes. With *Hope is a Prison,* she's created a heavy, vital accounting of intergenerational abuse that has the power to break your heart. It also has the power to redeem. The words of main protagonist, Liberty Zerillo, as she reflects on her journey of survival, "It's the simple acts of kindness that kept me alive," end this story with a glimmer of resonant light. It's the most that any of us can hope for."

-Wendy Rainey, Author of *Girl on the Highway*

"A grim tale with trash fairy overtones, Rebecca Schumejda's new chapbook, "*Hope is a Prison*," is at once chaotic and reasonable. The threads of the story may confuse at first, just as in this life. On closer reading, it's a chronicle of how one sin begets another, how a cloak of formal religion can conceal a bitter truth beneath. There's a confusion of blame, assistance, denial and finally, the horror of epiphany. The main narrator, a young girl named, "Liberty," is at anything but. She is surrounded by others equally damaged, equally hobbled. With lines like, "…stray cat husband who held my father like a feather between his teeth," this is Schumejda at the height of her considerable powers, understatement that softly wallops the reader. Jason Baldinger's grainy photos set the scene, with shots of decayed carousels and other signs of abandonment's loss. They reflect unfathomable serenity in the aftermath of the deeds described."

-Cheryl A. Rice, Author of *Love's Compass*

HOPE IS A PRISON

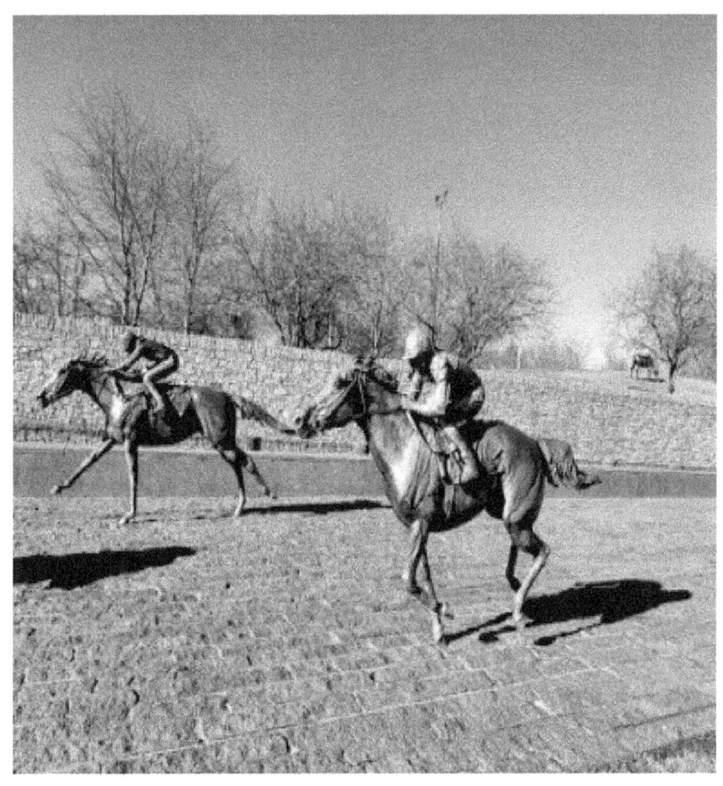

Poems by Rebecca Schumejda
Photos by Jason Baldinger

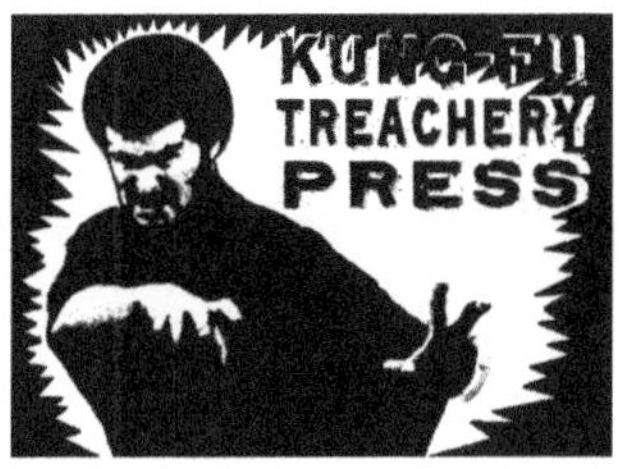

Kung Fu Treachery Press,

Rancho Cucamonga, California

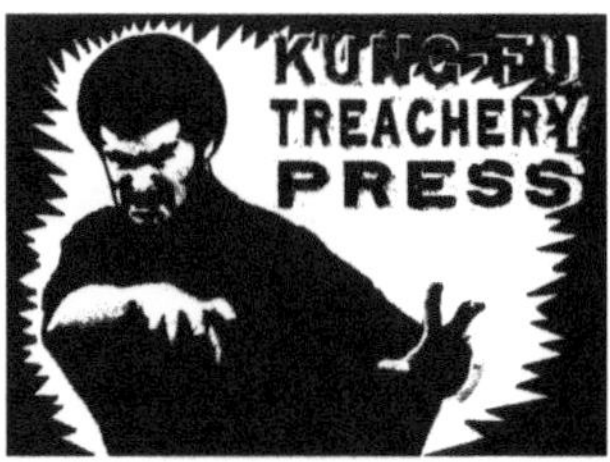

Copyright (c) Rebecca Schumejda, Jason Baldinger, 2024
First Edition 1 3 5 7 9 10 8 6 4 2
ISBN: 978-1-958182-78-9
LCCN: 2024942180

Author photos: Ed Crow
Cover photo: Youngstown, OH
Back Cover photo: Toledo, OH
Interior intro photo: Lexington, KY
Backpage photo: Bardstown, KY
All other photos: SCI Cresson, Cresson PA

Table of Contents

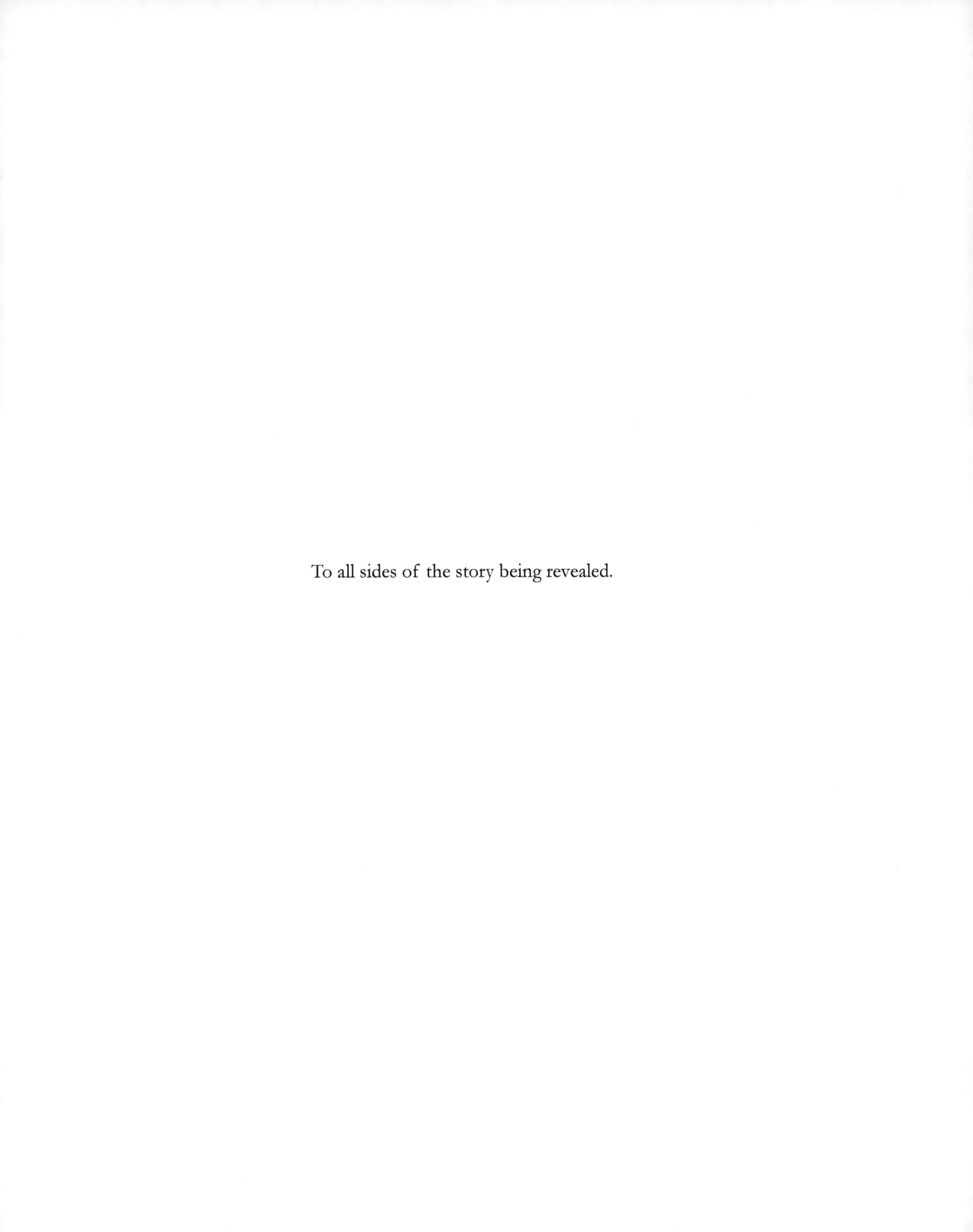

To all sides of the story being revealed.

Hope is a Prison

Before the Fall

Water drops race down the glass shower door
like horses running the circuit.
I root for my pick.
Since my family could barely afford rent,
equestrian lessons were out of the question;
but once I went with a friend,
sat outside a ring on a flimsy folding chair
and watched her trot a horse named Clover
around in circles.

"Libby I have to take a piss," my brother yells
while banging on the bathroom door.
I don't answer.
I focus on the warmth of the water,
scrubbing my skin red. I love the color of
thinking. My father began letting me
play hooky when I was in second grade,
brought me to the track,
his hand raced up my thigh like a jockey
approaching the finish line.
"Did you see that, did you see that?" my father asked,
slapping his hand print onto my thigh.
Every memory is a bruise
taking on unexpected shapes.

After my friend's riding lesson,
she handed me her helmet over the fence
so her mother could take a photo of
her blonde hair and Clover's mane
blowing in the wind.

I teetered on that folding chair–
my fingers, tiny hooves, galloping over
the soft velvety hill of someone else's life,
trying to steady myself before the fall.

Then the banging again and my brother
saying the same thing
he said right before he found out
about the secret,
"Libby, I am going to break this door down,
what are you doing in there?"
"Just go outside," I yell back.

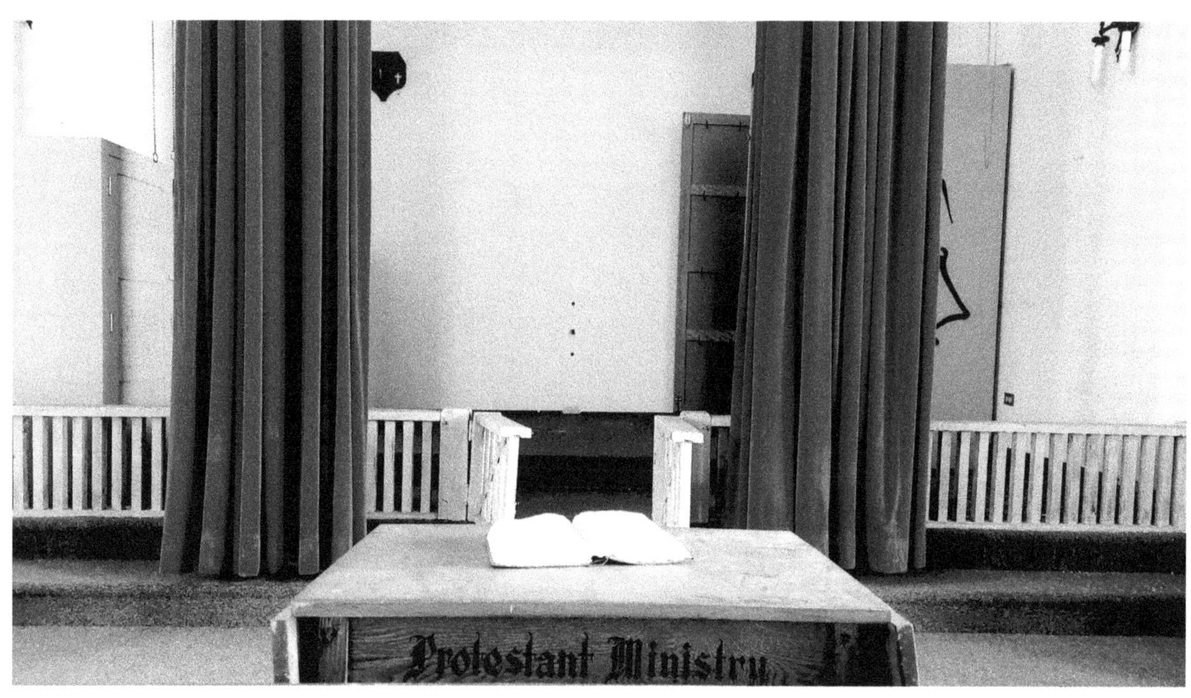
Protestant Ministry

Last Rites

The last time I heard my father's voice
was when my grandmother was transitioning in hospice.
We were gathered around her bed, saying our goodbyes,
when her son called collect from prison to encourage her
to ask for the Lord's forgiveness.

While death rattled in her throat,
I looked out the window,
a stray cat batted around a bluebird.
My grandmother dismissed religion
long before I was born
but kept a crucifix in her nightstand drawer.
She had a stray cat husband, who held my father
like a feather between his teeth.

She looked out of the same window
then at me as my father yammered on about redemption.
Or maybe she didn't look out the window,
maybe I just wanted her to.
The last time she spoke directly to me
was the day before her son was sentenced.
"Just tell the truth, that he didn't really hurt you,"
she begged, "just tell the truth."

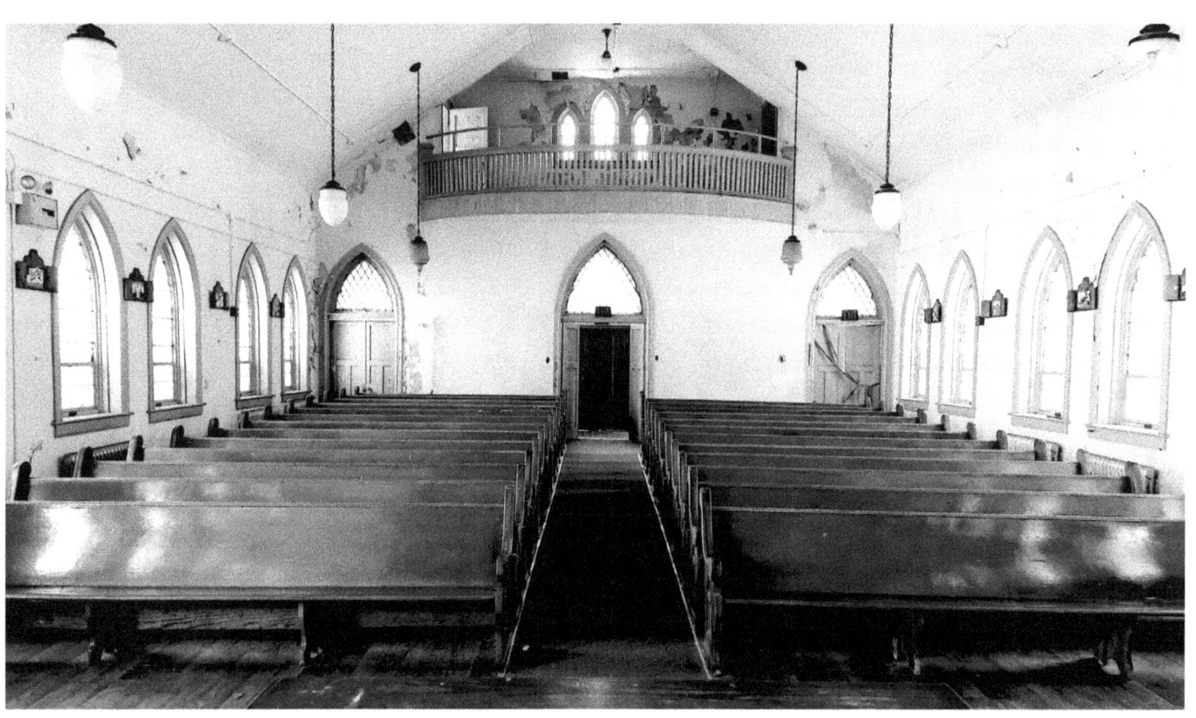

Lessons

Another time my father let me play hooky,
he brought me to an empty church.
We sat on a pew toward the middle.
He handed me a bible and told me to read.

Everytime, I mispronounced a word
he thrust his fingers deep inside of me.
When I cried, he told me to blame
my teachers for not doing their jobs.

I held the bible as if a horse's reins.

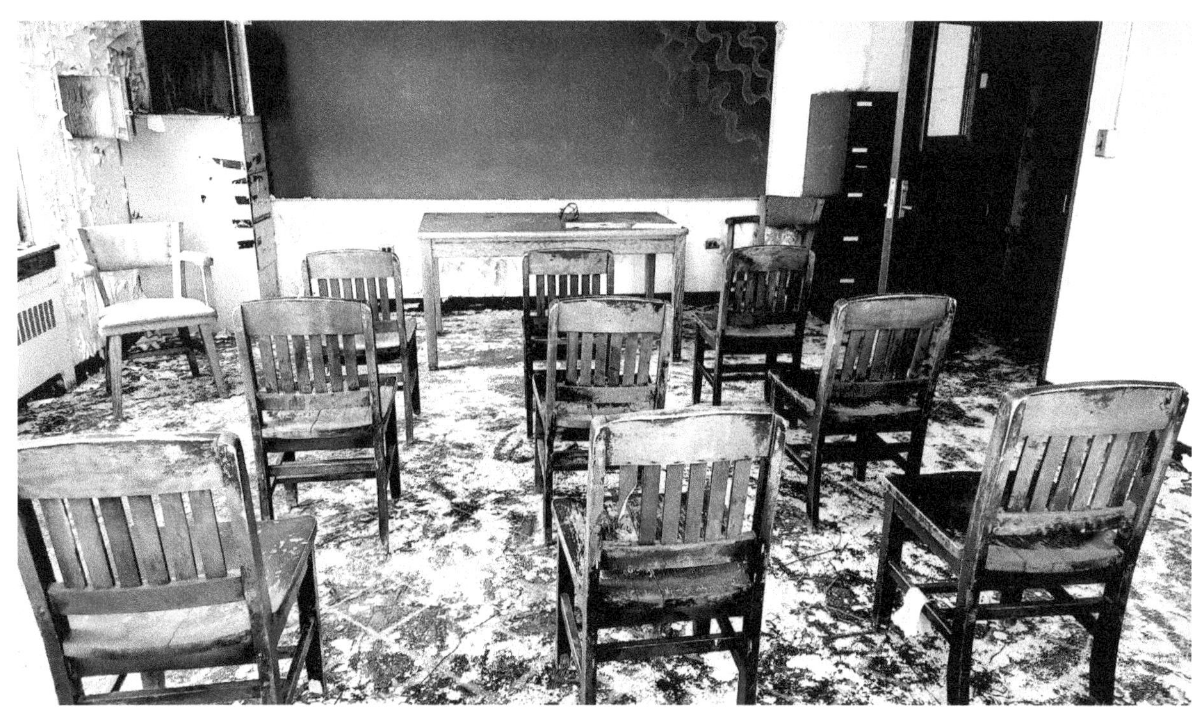

Help

"Liberty
Liberty
Liberty Zerillo
It's your turn to read," my third grade teacher, Mrs. Pinski, demanded
standing over my desk.

I froze, hoping she would move on, but she didn't.

"Take out your book, Liberty," she directed me.
When I did as I was told,
she saw the bruises on my wrists and arms:
blue, purple, black, yellow, green mosaics.

"Angela, can you continue reading?" she asked the girl sitting behind me.

She put her hand on my back   I flinched
leaned down   and I started to feel warm and dizzy
"Come out into the hallway," she whispered   I stood up
she stepped forward   my legs gave out
she reached out to catch me   but I hit the ground before she could.

In the nurse's office,   My teacher left
I was berated with questions   and came back with my lunch—
one after the other,   a piece of stale bread
I asked for my sandwich.   wrapped in the Sunday funnies.

"How?" she asked
throwing my lunch into the trash
in front of me.
I lunged into the trash can
and grabbed it.

"Oh, Liberty, no,   While she was gone,
I will get you something else."   I closed my eyes   There was
whispering.   to stop the tears.
My teacher brought back   There were footsteps.
a tray of food, a sandwich,   I could see the words.
an apple, a bag of chips,   I closed my eyes
two milks.   and there were the words   from that Bible
blurring.
                    I mispronounced words
        I knew; it was my fault.

Maybe I liked being hurt.
Maybe I asked for it.
Maybe I wanted it.

Two new people
and more of the same
questions. I missed music
and recess. When the bell rang,
they put me on the bus
and just like that
I went home.

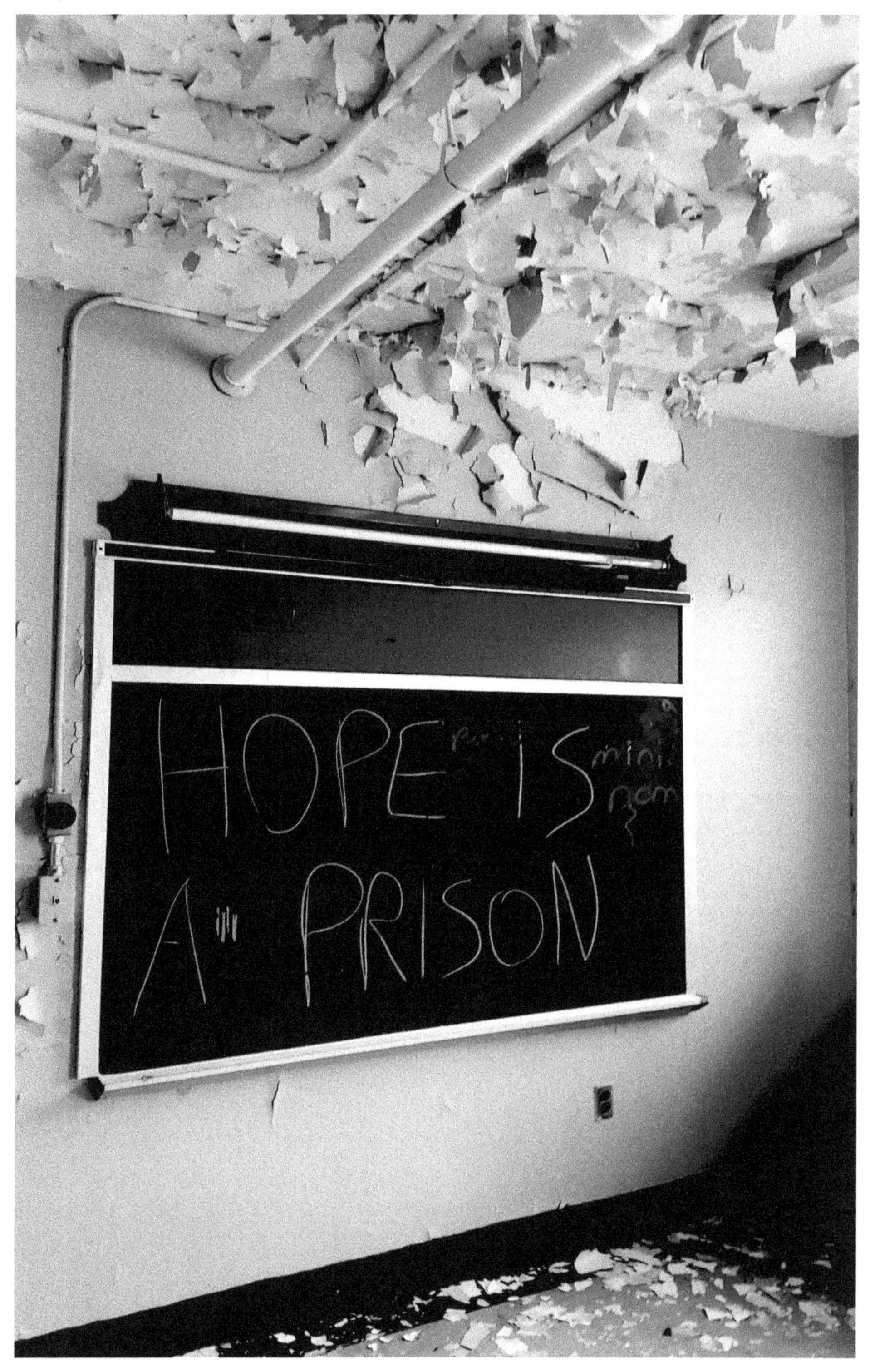

HOPE IS
A PRISON

The Hole in my Backyard

Before they got me on the bus,
the younger of the two women, who questioned me last
promised that it would all be over soon.
The older woman elbowed her gently.

I held onto hope for a few days
until afterschool on Friday.
My mother was waiting
in the living room when I got off the bus.
I could hear my brothers in the backyard.
They were probably playing baseball
with the broom handle and a pair of rolled-up, dirty socks.

You lying slut, she said, *you stupid, lying slut.*

After that no one looked at me.
There were no more sandwiches wrapped in the Sunday funnies.
Since no one believed me, my father became more brazen,
he didn't have to bring me to the track or to the church anymore.
All he had to do was close a door behind us.
People stop asking questions
when they don't want to know the answers.

Everyday at school, I was given hot lunch. Sometimes
Mrs. Pinsky would leave something in my desk—
a plastic bag filled with cookies, a pair of winter gloves,
a roll of quarters, a deck of cards, a small teddy bear,
a brand new paperback copy of the Black Beauty.

When the gifts began to pile up, I placed everything
nonperishable into a shoebox,
dug a hole in my backyard
and buried my hope
so no one could steal it from me.

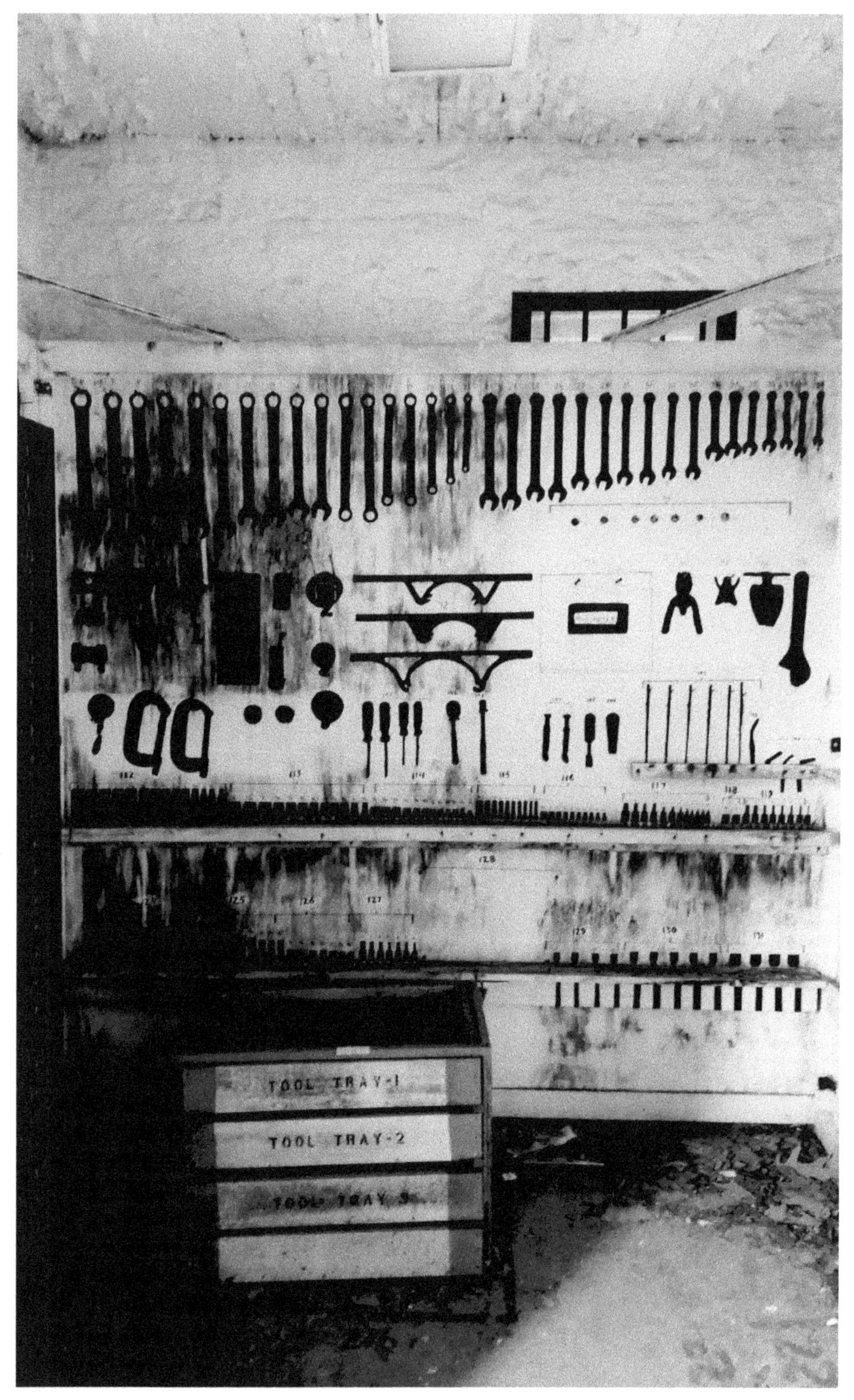

18

Acquiring Tools

What Liberty doesn't understand is that she has it easy.
I didn't have a mother or a father. I lived with my aunt and uncle.
When my uncle said go grab me a wrench he meant bend over
his workbench; a screwdriver meant open your legs;
a clamp meant keep your mouth shut.

My aunt stayed in the house, placed lace doilies over hard surfaces.
When she said I was lucky he taught me how to fix broken things
she meant you're on your own. When she said wash your hands
before sitting down to eat she meant don't bring the truth to the table;
when we bowed our heads before a meal and my uncle said grace
it meant be thankful; it could always be worse.

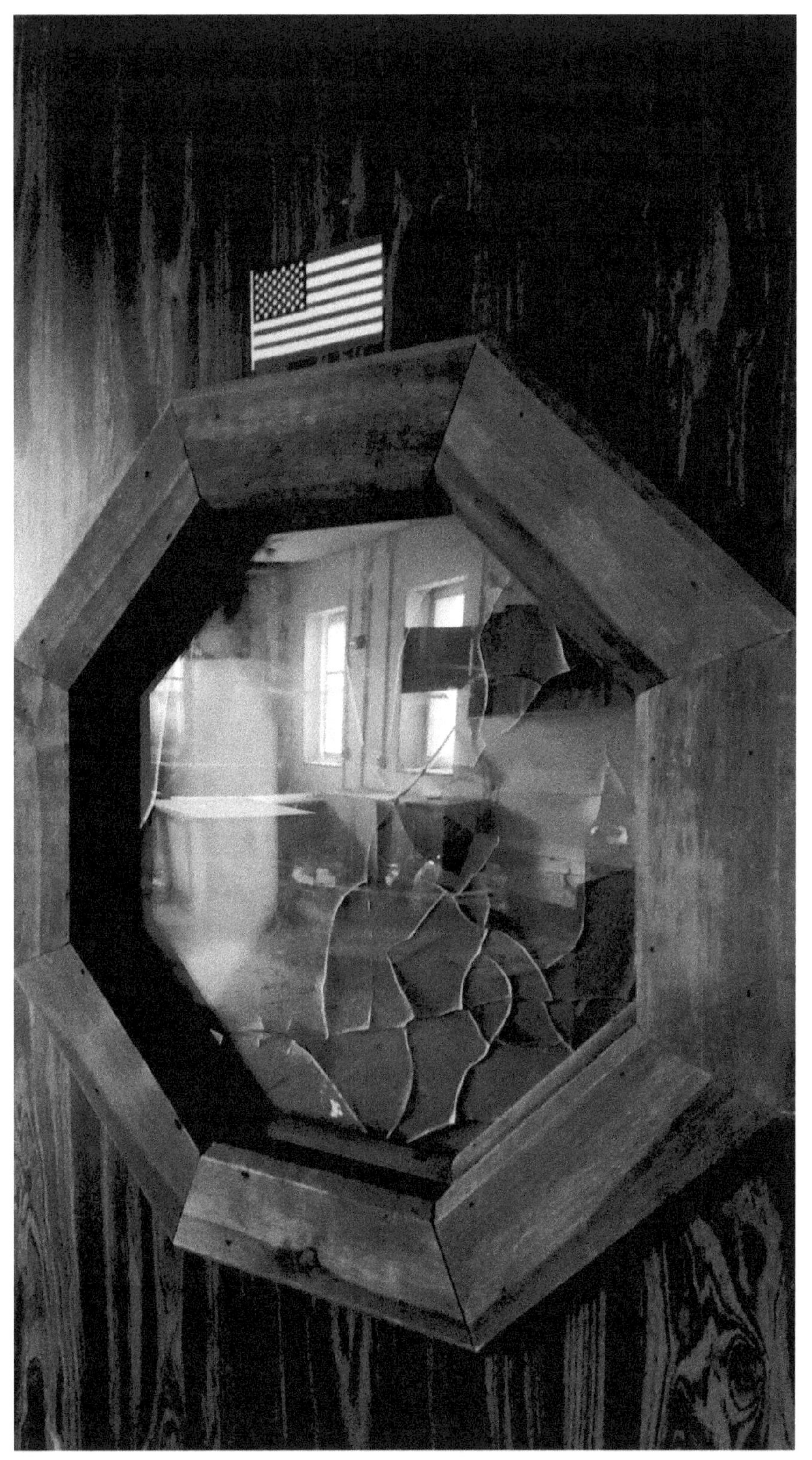

What We Deserve

If he did what Libby said he did,
he did it because she let him—
she always hangs around him, begging for
attention so she got what she wanted.

If he did what Libby said he did,
CPS won't pay the rent, they won't
put food on our table, clothes on our backs.
Take Libby, I told the lady who asked all
the questions, who looked at me like trash.
Take her if she wants to go.

My aunt sewed me a dress adorned with
tiny roses and lace trim. When she found
it ripped and stained with oil, I tried
to tell her about the lessons I was learning
in the garage. She didn't want to hear
instead she made me put the dress on
and sit in front of a mirror.
This, she said, *is what little girls
who deserve what they get, look like.*

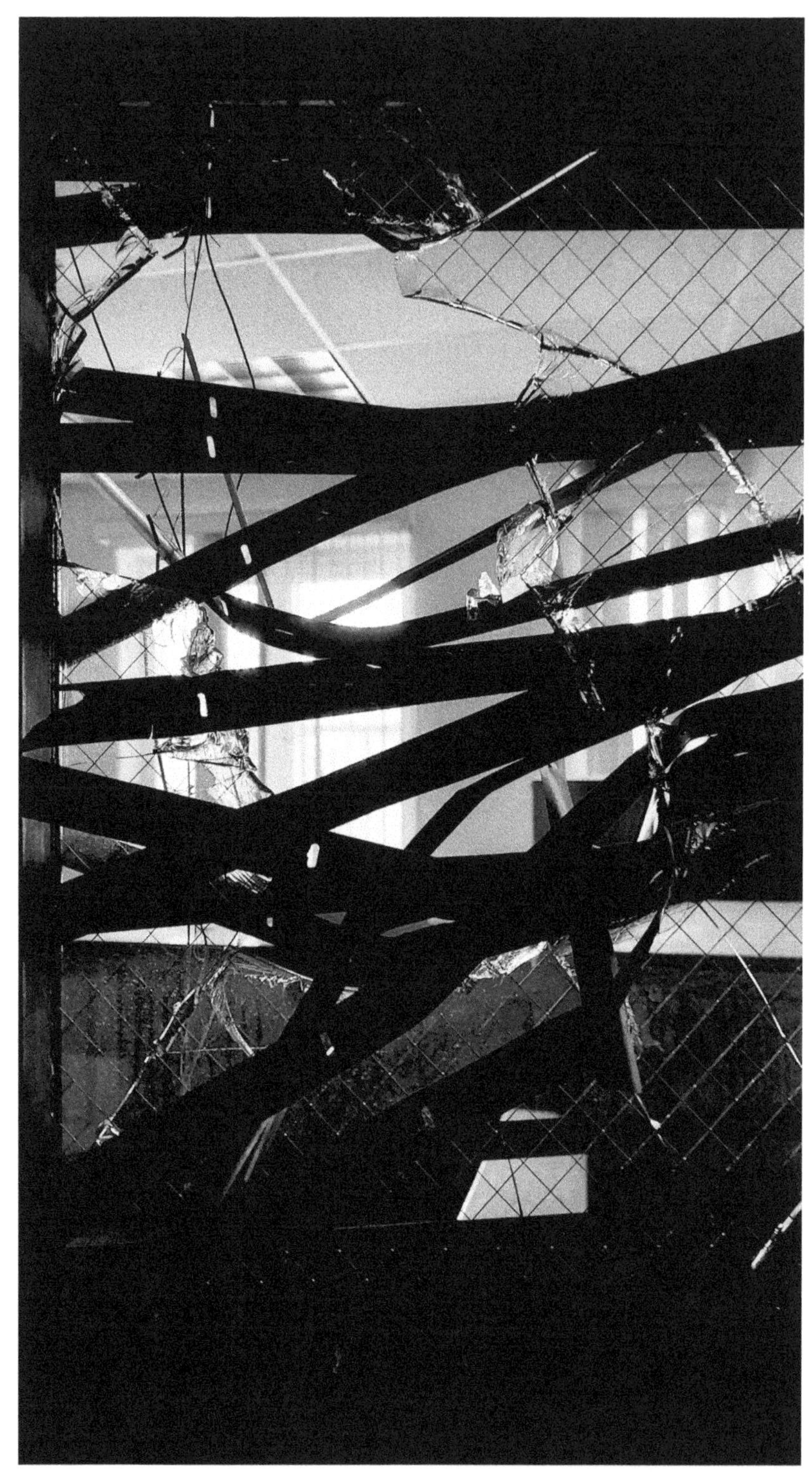

When "No!" Doesn't Mean Stop,
It Means It Never Happened.

When I finally told my mother
about the race track,
how his fingers galloped up my thigh,
she said, *You went willingly.*
She said *I told you to stay in school,
look at what happened to me?*

Then she turned away,
walked down the hall
into her bedroom,
slammed the door.
I heard glass shatter.
I heard her scream
No!

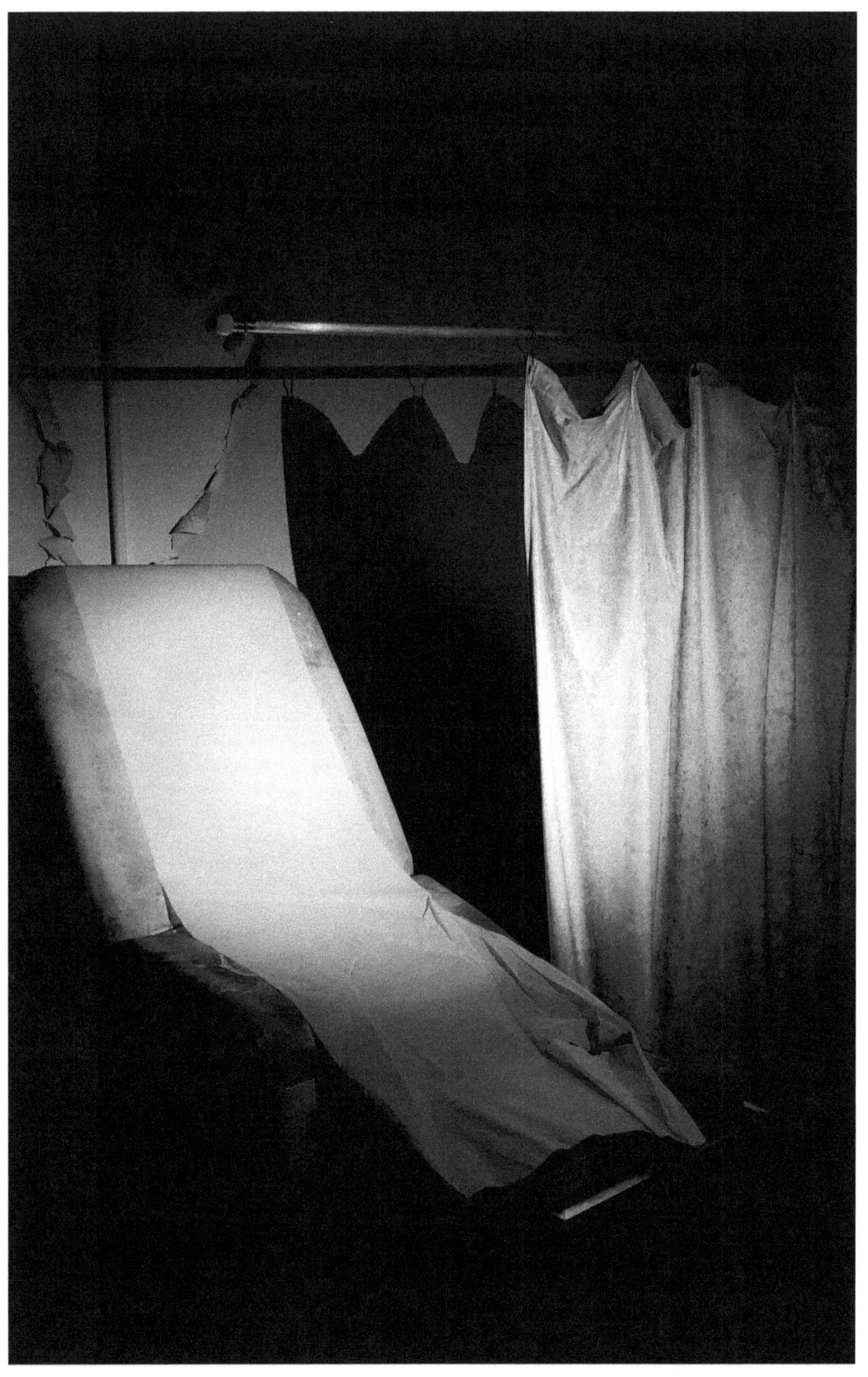

Choices

There was a curtain in the room—
the kind used for a shower
to keep the water from splashing out.

The doctor, who wasn't really a doctor,
or maybe he was but he didn't seem like one,
said we can get rid of it right now.

My uncle was outside the door.
He was pacing back and forth.
I asked to use the bathroom first.

In the bathroom, there was a small window
that I squeezed out of one life through
and into the next.

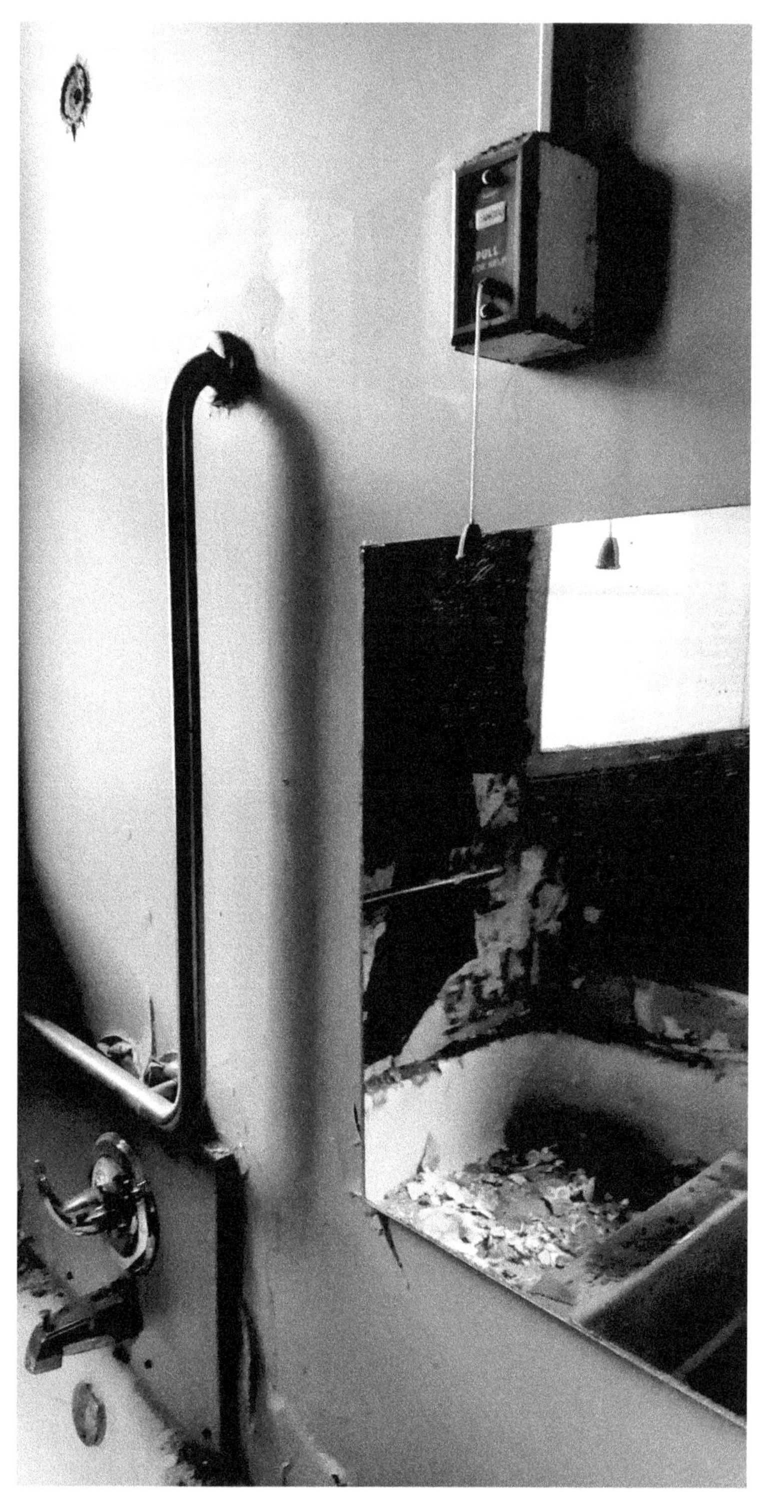

Found

For a few weeks, I slept in a tub at an abandoned house
a few towns away from my aunt and uncle's.

It's easy to hide when no one is looking for you.

I met Joe when I was panhandling. He asked,
What's a pretty girl like you doing begging for anything?

He took me back to his place and I never left.

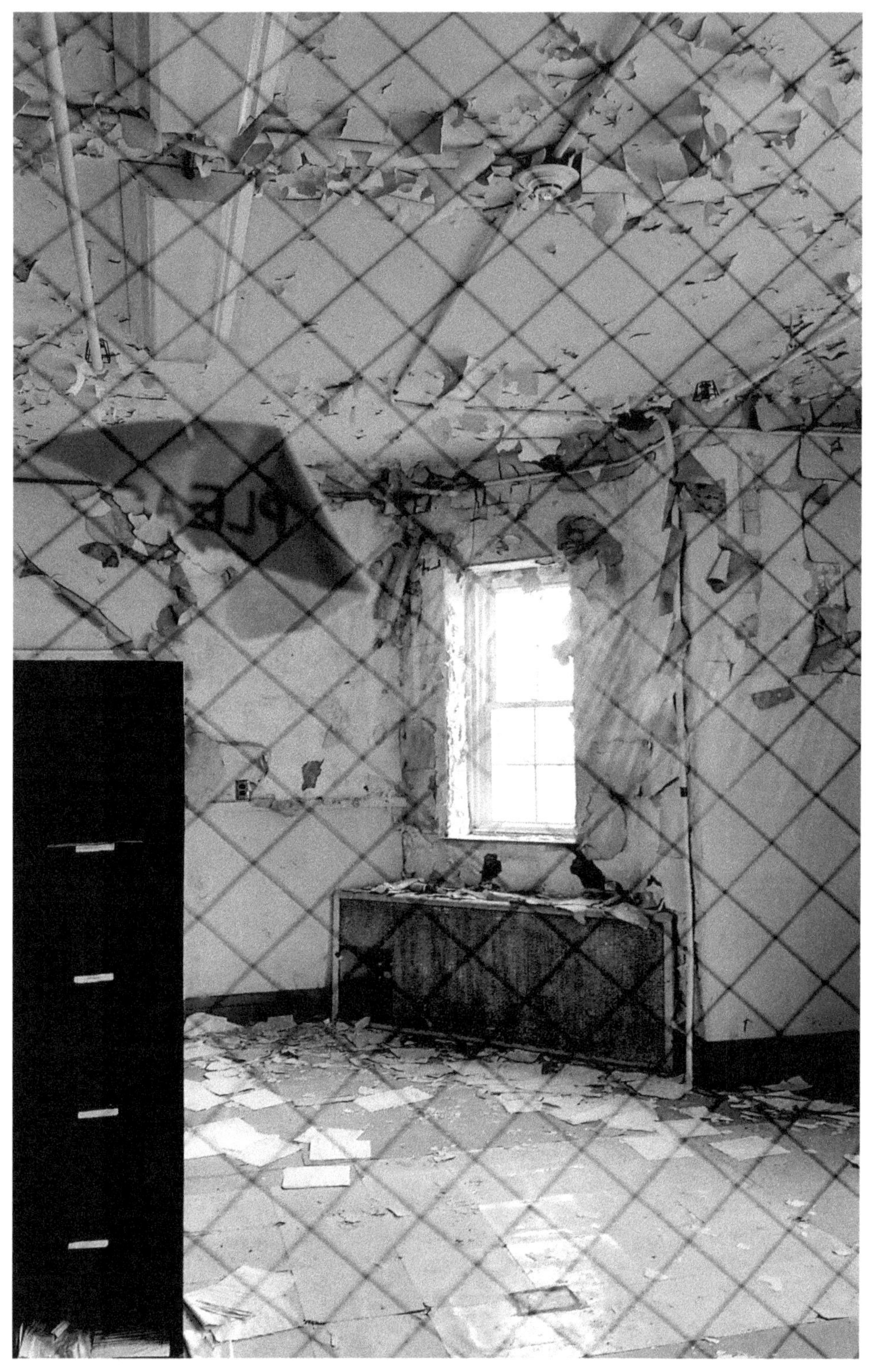

In My Womb

Paint peeled,
dust and debris accumulate.
There is a window
without a shade;
someone painted that window shut.
if you look out the window
there is a tree.

Sometimes a bird perches on a limb
sometimes disappears
sometimes a nest
sometimes tiny fragile eggs
sometimes he comes in
shhhh…
sometimes he asks if he makes me happy
sometimes I say yes

and he promises
that he will get around to painting
when I clean up this mess.
Once I saw my youngest brother
outside climbing the tree.
He reached into the nest,
took out an egg
and tossed it across the yard
like a stone skipped across the surface of a lake.

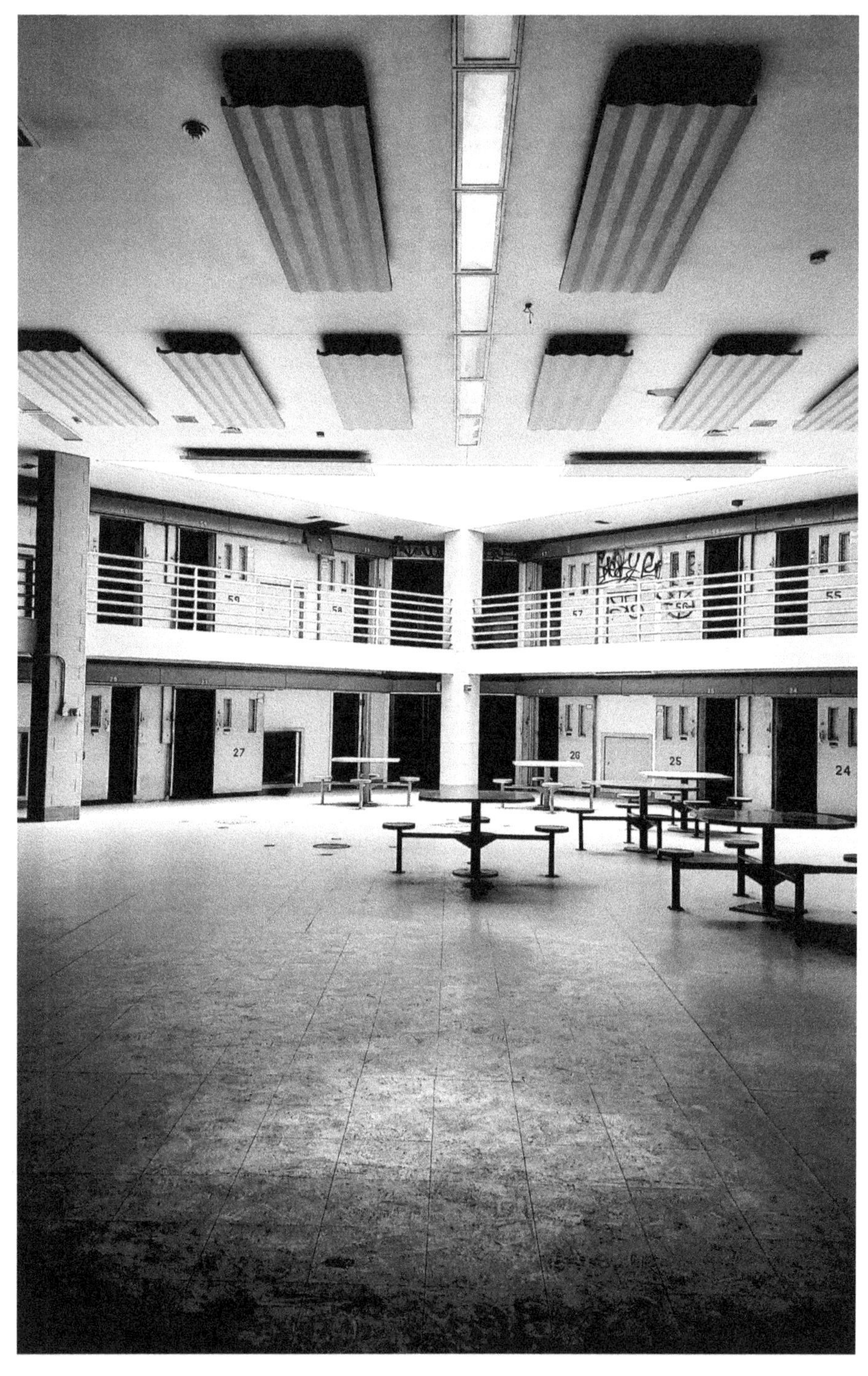

Lunch Trays

In the cafeteria,

I feel safer alone,

facing a windowless wall

eating everything on my tray.

One day, a crater faced boy

sits down across from me

and asks me how I am.

I don't say anything so

he talks about his pet—

a crested gecko, named Dip.

When the bell rings,

he says it was nice talking to you.

The next day he comes back,

and talks about his mom—

he didn't have a dad, but that is ok

because it has to be and

when the bell rings,

he picks up my lunch tray

slides it under his and takes it back for me.

That following Monday,
he talks about how he wants
to be a pro-wrestler and about
his favorite teacher, Mrs. Pinsky.
That Tuesday, he tells me his mom
waits tables at the diner and he
goes in after school,
sits at the counter and drinks an egg cream.

After a few weeks, I tell him
I love horses and the next day
he gives me a plastic white pegasus figurine.

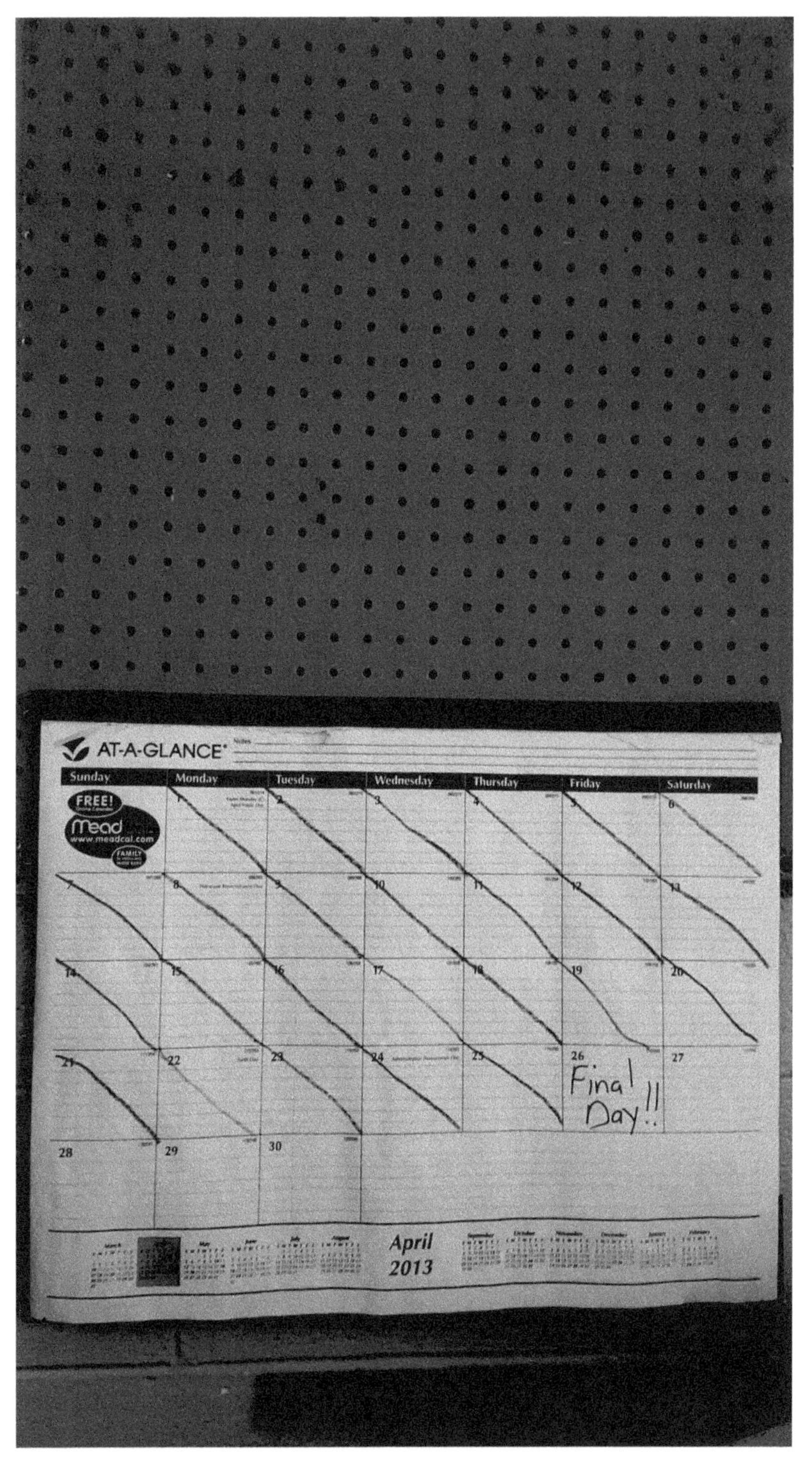

AT-A-GLANCE®
Sunday
Monday
Tuesday
Wednesday
Thursday
Friday
Saturday
FREE!
mead
www.meadcal.com
Final
Day!!
April
2013

The Last Day of Freedom

On the last day of school,
I find a public library card
with my name on it
and a pink heart-shaped sticky note
with the words *Don't give up*
written in perfect cursive.

When the bell rings,
I let everyone go out before me.
When I get to the door,
I wrap my arms around Mrs. Pinsky's waist.
She smells sweet like candy or roses.
I look up at her and a few raindrops
fall on my cheeks and run down my face.
If I didn't have a bus to catch,
I would hold on to her forever.

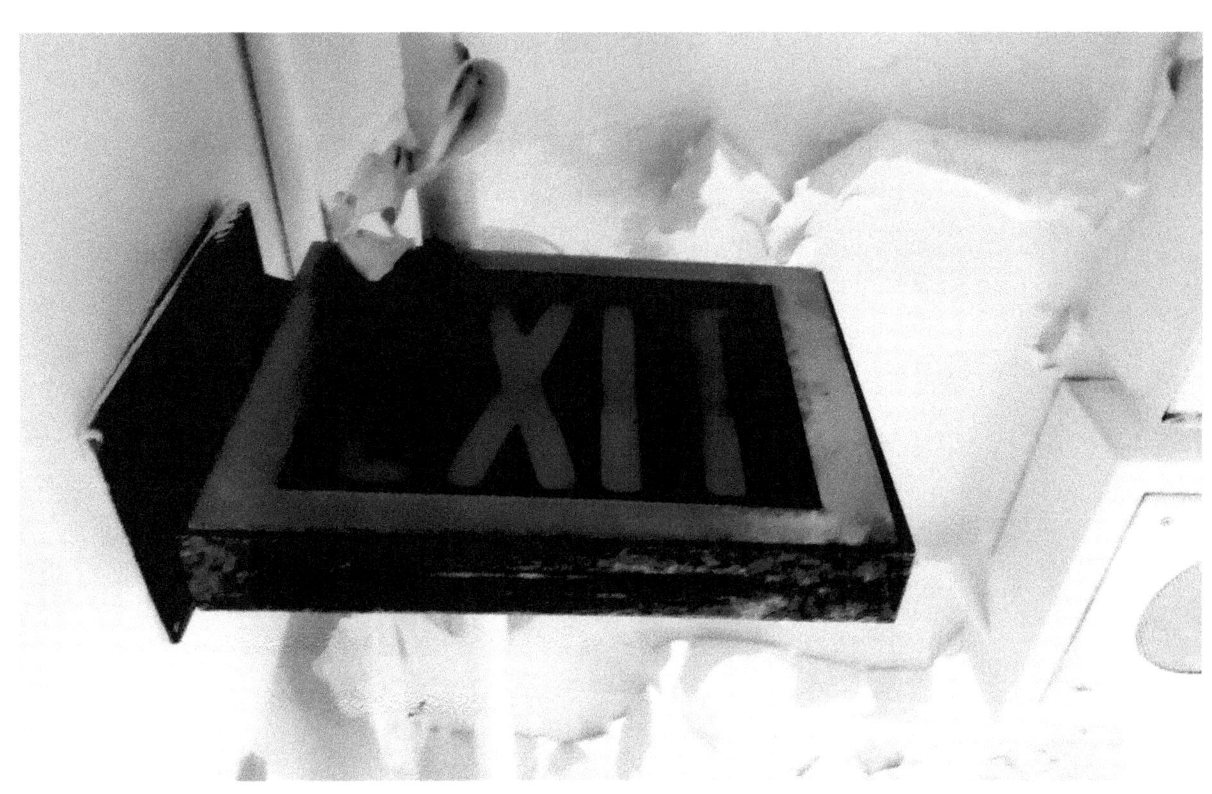
EXIT

The First Day of Summer Break

I could have held Libby forever
taken her far away, saved her
from her daily torture.
I couldn't even sit in the nurse's office
and listen to the horrific details of her abuse.

And then the promise, the let down–
Not enough evidence, there's nothing we can do.

Nothing?

    Nothing.

So, she is stuck there?

    Yes, for now.

But, I don't understand. How?

    There is not enough evidence
    and family members protect one another.

We called again one day when Libby came in
and could barely sit down. The stories she told
were even more vile.

After the same outcome, Libby begged me
not to call again. She said the calls made it worse,
that the calls gave that monster more confidence.

How could a father do that to his child?

How could a mother let that happen?

I hold my belly and promise the child
growing inside of me that I will protect her;

my belly can forever be her umbrella.

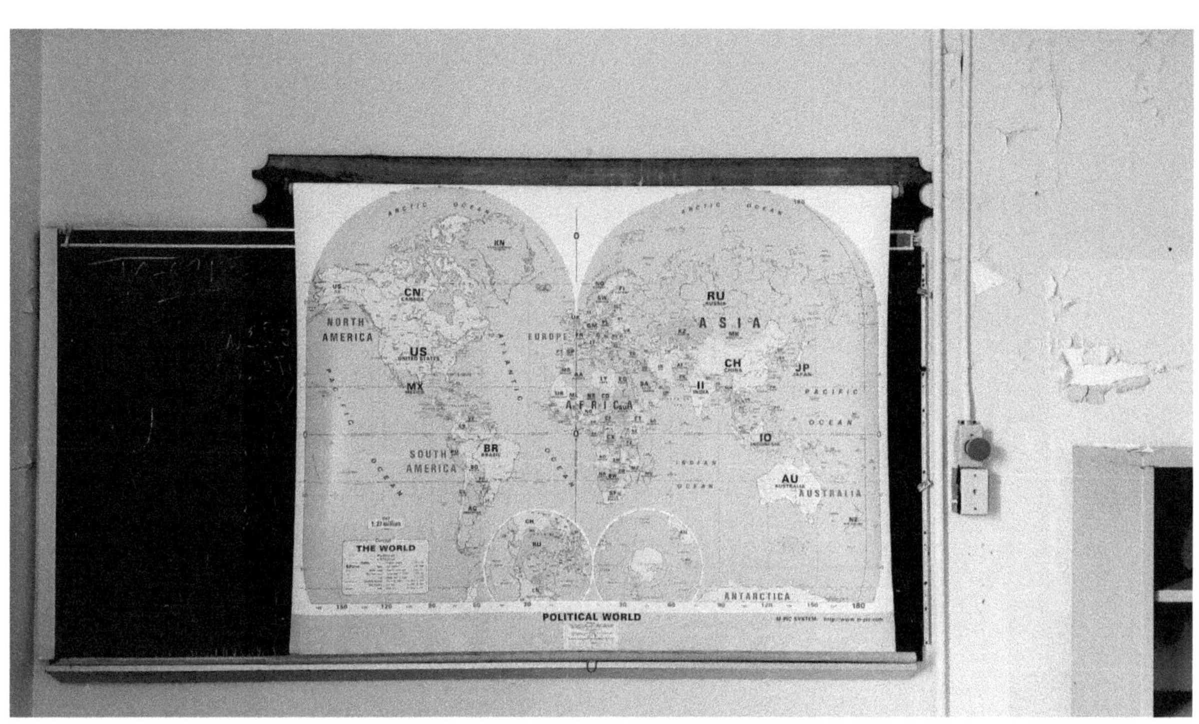
NORTH
AMERICA
SOUTH
AMERICA
ASIA
AFRICA
AUSTRALIA
ANTARCTICA
ARCTIC OCEAN
ARCTIC OCEAN
PACIFIC
OCEAN
PACIFIC
OCEAN
INDIAN
OCEAN
ATLANTIC
OCEAN
EUROPE
US
CN
MX
BR
RU
CH
JP
AU
THE WORLD
POLITICAL WORLD
M-PIC SYSTEM

Anywhere

Mrs. Pinsky was right,
you can travel anywhere in a book
and the librarians are so nice.
Sometimes I get there before
they do and I leave with them
carrying a handful of books.

I visit The Eiffel Tower,
the Great Wall, The Pyramids,
the Kremlin, The Louvre,
and even Ancient Rome.

But my favorite place is still
galloping through fields
on horseback, the wind lifting
the pain away.

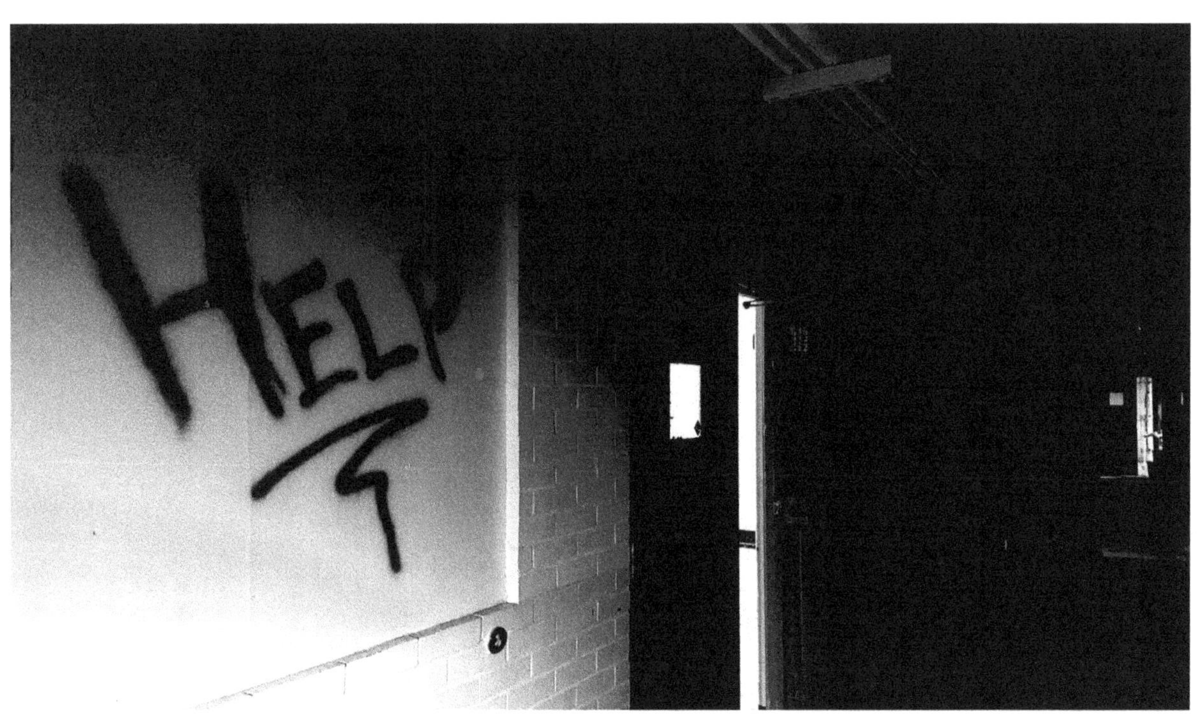

HELP

Help

Help mocks me for years,
makes promises it can't keep,
gifts me hope then steals it back
over and over again.

Two days after my father
was sentenced, I run into
Mrs. Pinsky and her daughter
at the library. I tell her help
finally came. She stares at
my blossoming belly and
I know she wants to ask
but doesn't want to know.

I tell her that even after
help came, I am unsure if
it will make my life better
or worse. The laws are
funny that way.

As I am leaving,
Mrs. Pinsky's daughter
hands me a bookmark
that she decorated
during story time.
I hold onto it as I watch them
walk out of the library doors—
and into the rain without an umbrella.

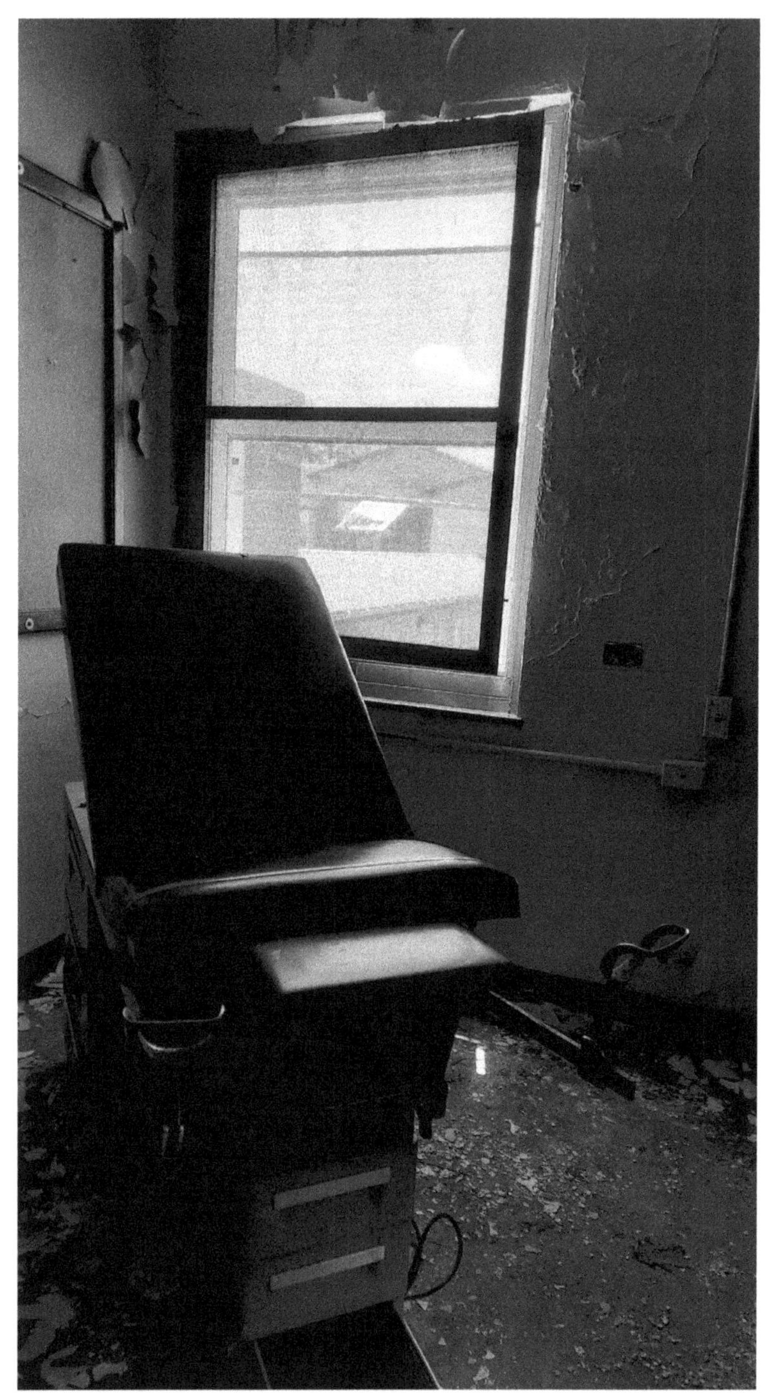

My Choice

I stare at the ultrasound image
of his child growing inside me.
Can you hear that? The doctor aks,
That's the baby's heartbeat. Even though,
the doctor knows the story behind
my situation, he is sincerely excited.

You have the gift of life inside of you,
he says, *the most precious gift of all.*
He tells me my choices are limited
because the father isn't my father,
biologically, and the Supreme Court's
recent ruling impacted the laws.
You can keep the child he says
approvingly *or you can give it away,*
he says with a frown, *that's your choice.*

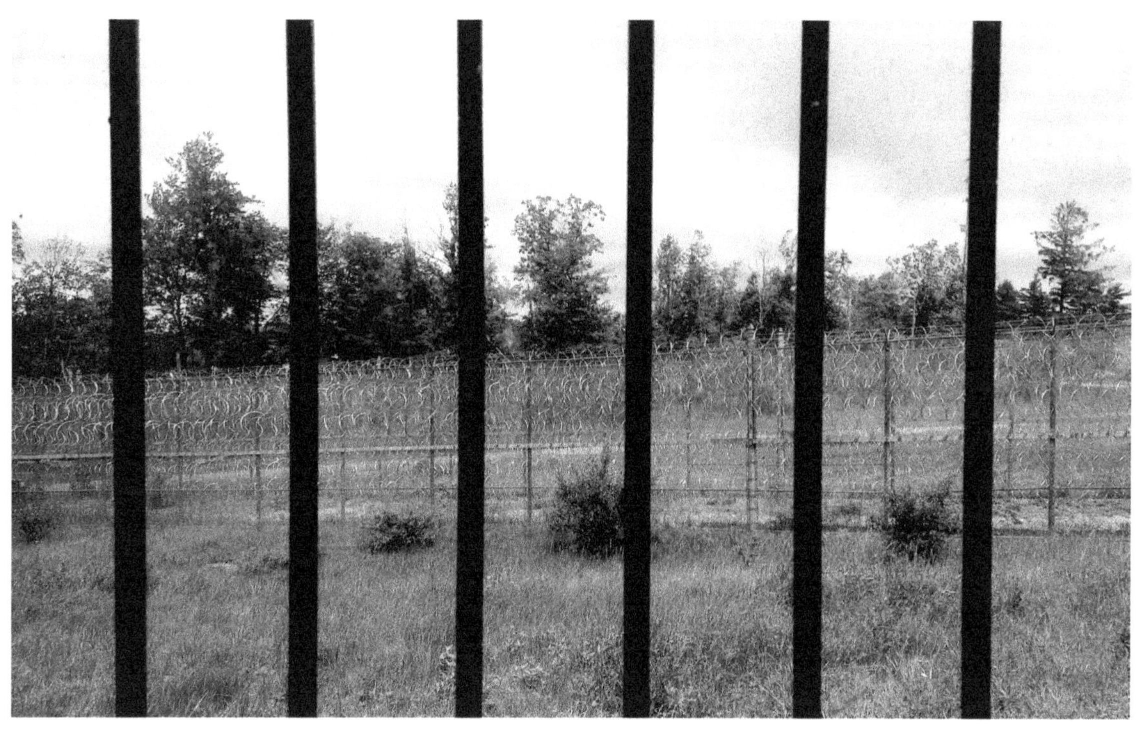

After Help Came

How could you do this to us? You're a lying slut, my mother screams.
My brothers, his biological sons, don't look at me or speak to me,
but sometimes they hand me letters he writes me from prison.
Letters where he writes *I forgive you, but now it is time to ask God*
for forgiveness or *You can still tell the truth* or *I'll be out before*
our baby can talk. My mother tells me she hopes that I have a little girl
so that she can do to me what I did to her. I hold my fingers
like bars over my belly. I hold my barbed wire anger in, I hold it all in.

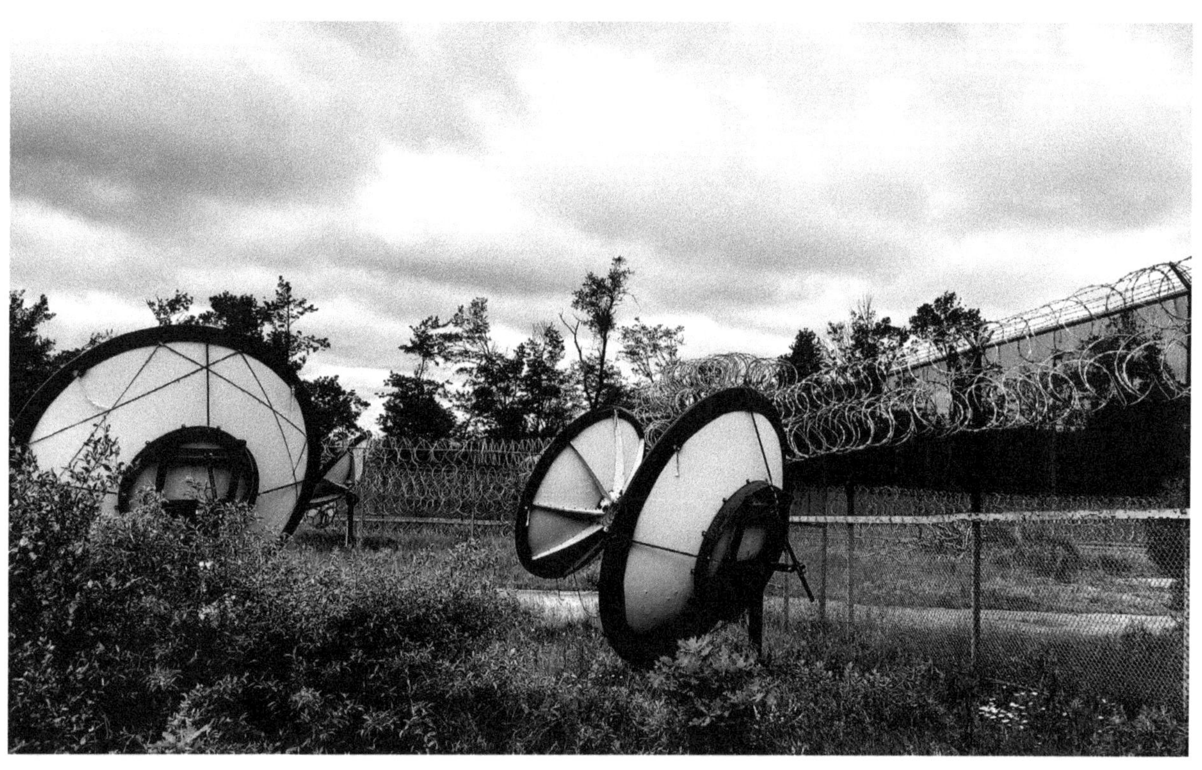

Mine

And even from inside he still has power over me–
bars, barbed-wires and locks can't save me.

I still feel his touch, his hand over my mouth,
his warm breath on my neck, *You are mine,* he says

as if I were a horse, as if he holds the reins and gets to
direct me where he wills. *No matter where you go,*

I will find you, he promises. I place a stack of library
books in my bag. On the bookmark a small offering,

the number of an organization that helps girls like me.
I tuck it in between the pages of a book about the galaxy

and ontop I place a few changes of clothes. Someone
will meet me at the airport, someone will hand me

a ticket, an itinerary, an opportunity for release.
Someone will risk their freedom to give me mine.

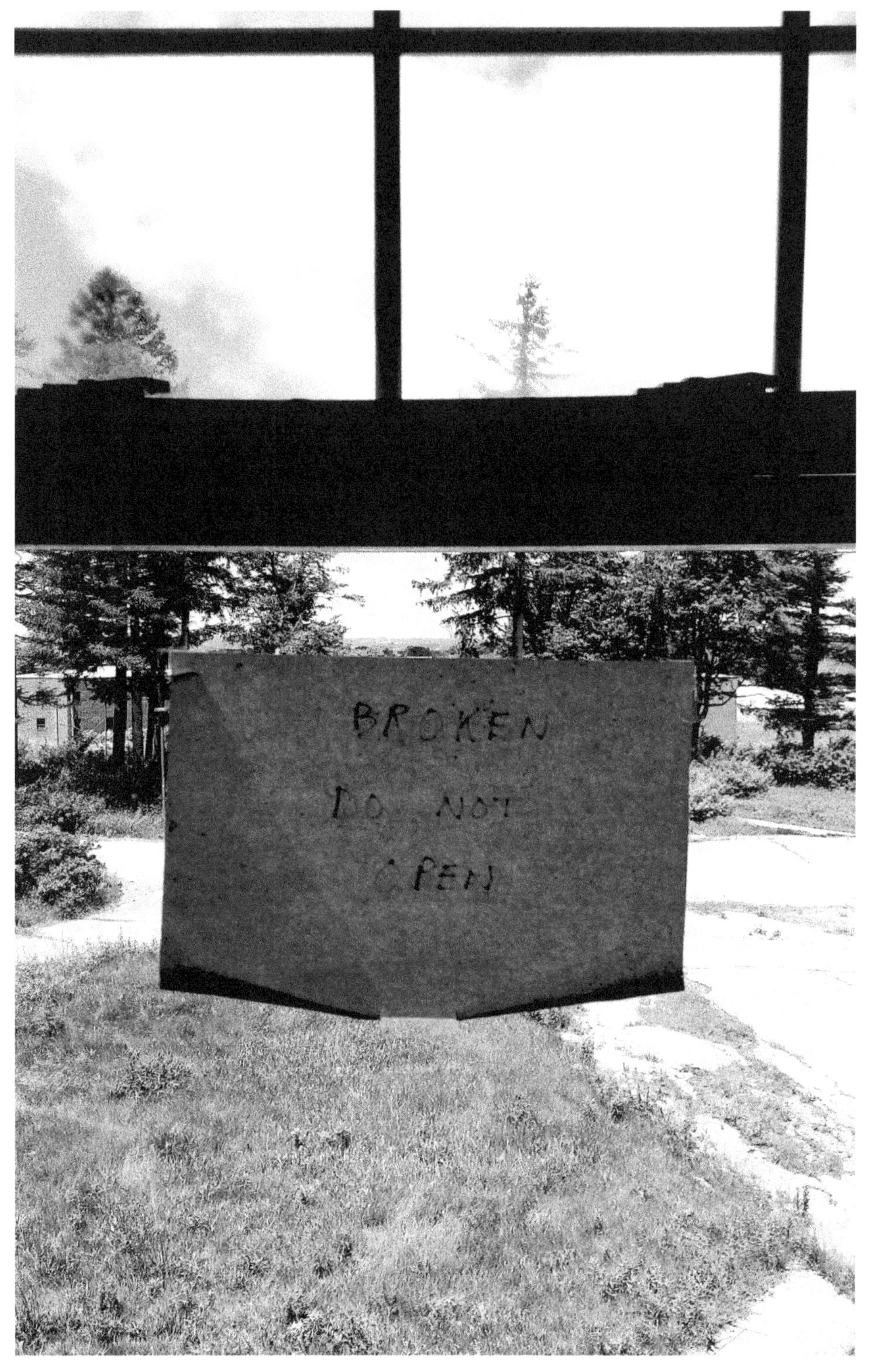

50

Broken Do Not Open

I ask the man, wearing a business suit,
sitting next to me on the plane
how to open the window.
He chuckles, tells me about air pressure,
and then asks me where I am from, where I am going.

I recite the story I was handed in the terminal
by a woman who told me
I was not alone.

Interesting, the man says, convinced by my ability
to deceive. I add to the story, talk about my horse,
Clover, how I miss her already.

I look out the window and think maybe I am not broken,
maybe the pressure inside me is just higher right now.

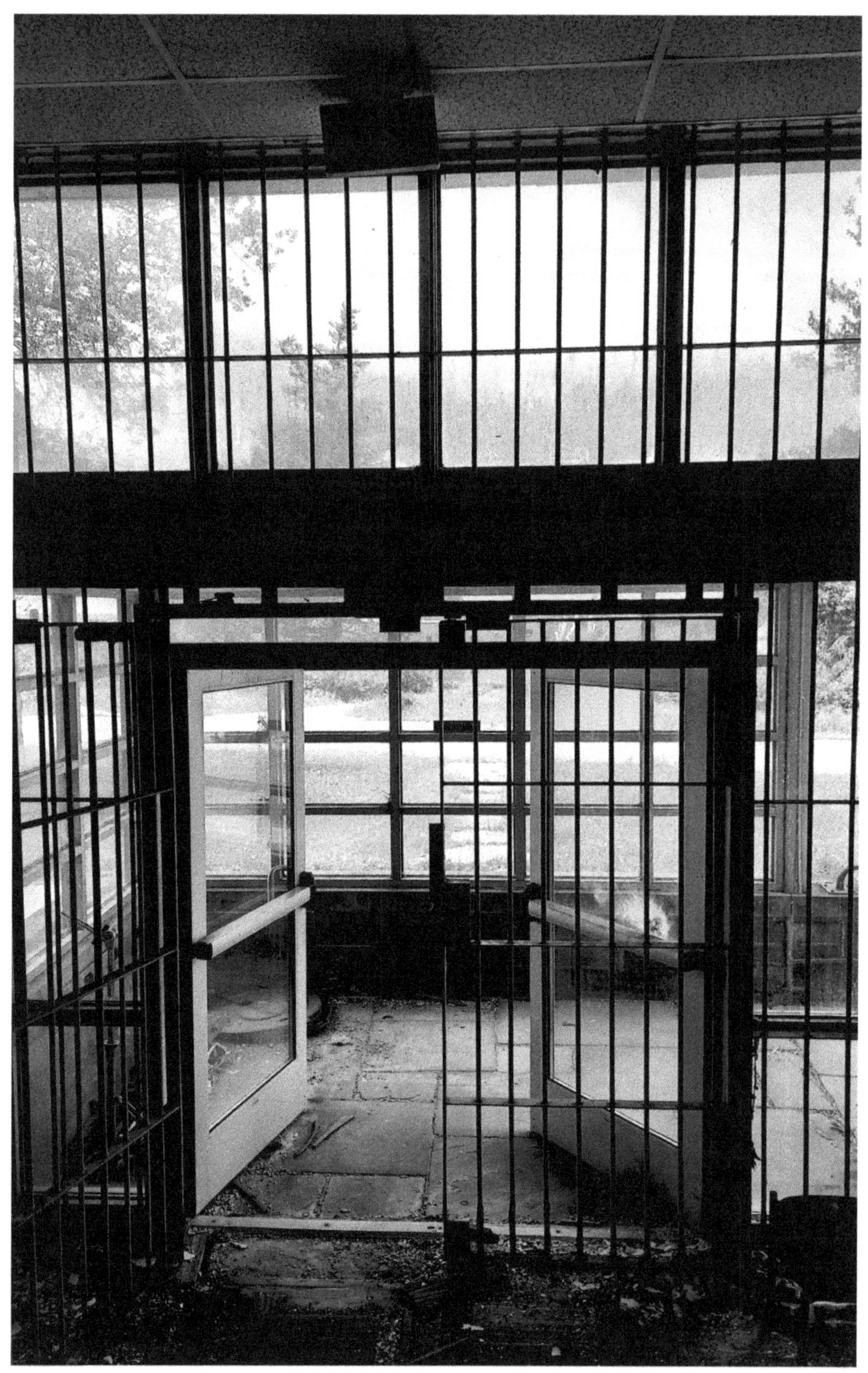

Your Daughter

When I ask him if he did what she says he did—
he looks above my head, smiles, says,
Come on baby, would I ever do something
like that to your daughter?

I know she is telling the truth
not because he can't look at me or because
he has tears in his eyes but because
Liberty suddenly became my daughter, not ours.

Five years after I left home, I ran into my Uncle
at a gas station. He cornered me by the gas pump
and when he saw Liberty in the backseat,
he said, *Boy, she sure does look like you.*

Sitting across from my husband now,
in the state prison's visiting room,
I see my Uncle's eyes looking through me—
trying to figure out how to get inside, how to stay.

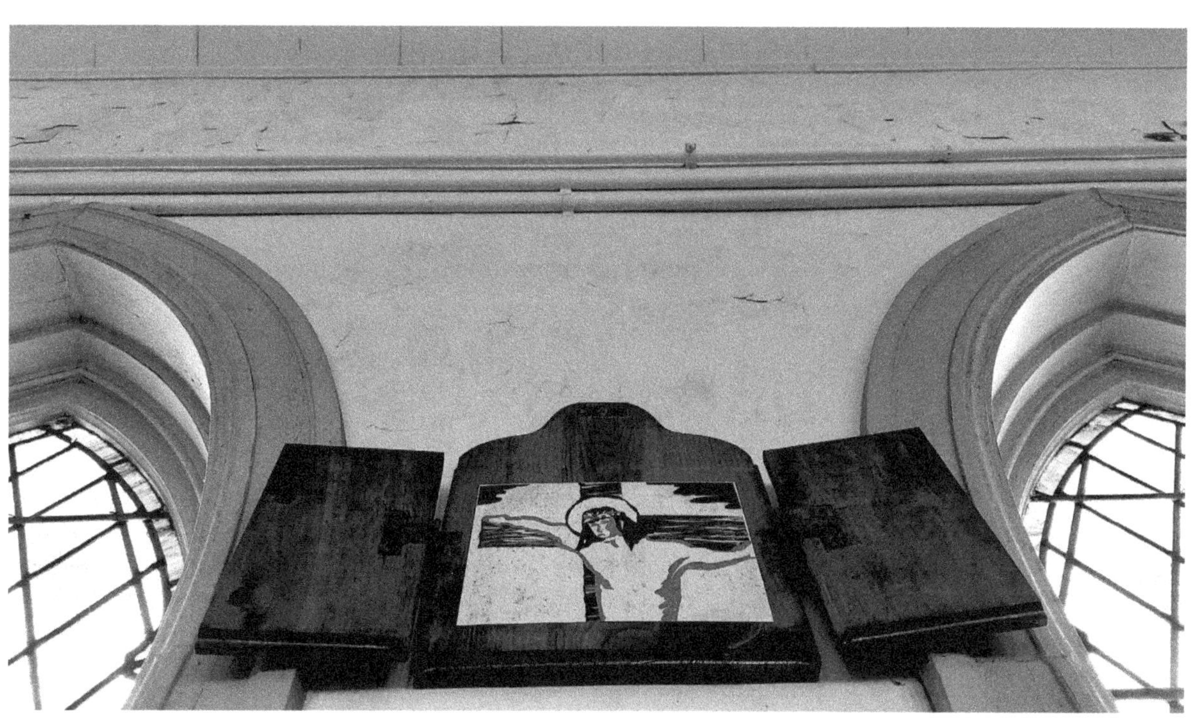

Swarm

When visiting time is over,
he opens his arms
and I let him wrap himself around me–
my body has become a swarm of honey bees
that have outgrown their home.
I stay there until the guards
begin to become uneasy.

Oh God, Liberty, what have I done?

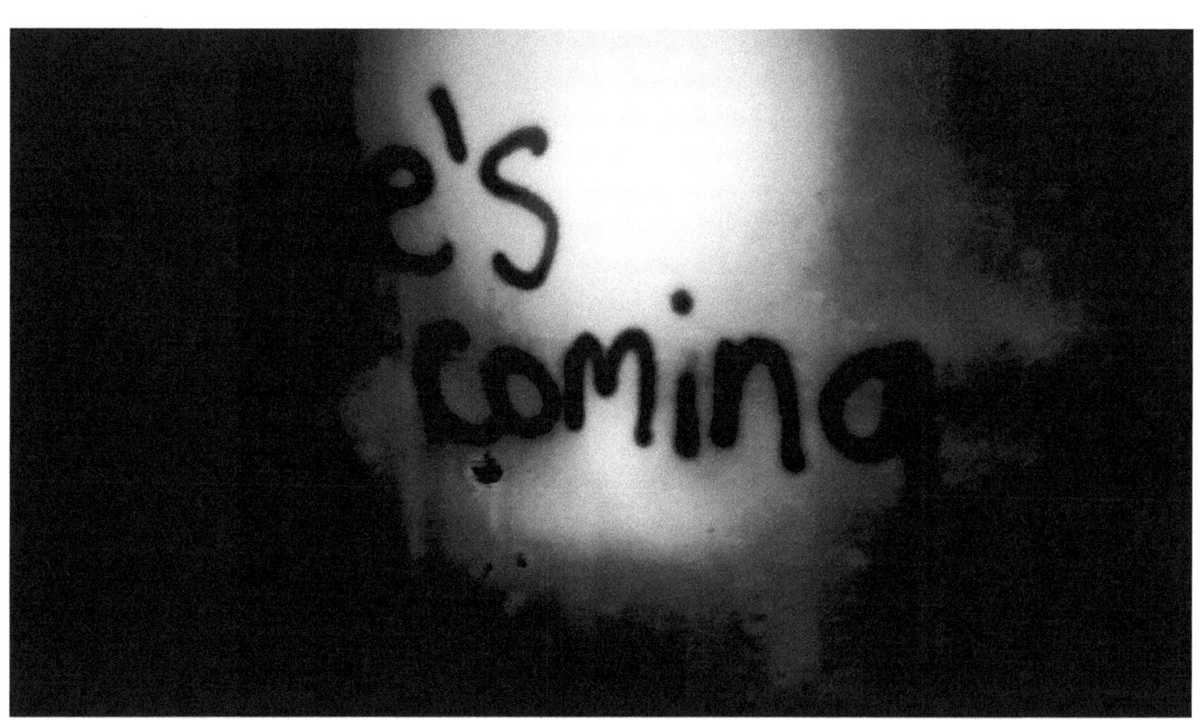

e's
coming

Warnings

The last time I went to church,
I bounced Liberty on my leg,
Joe sat beside us
and our first born son
slept in his carseat on the pew
on the otherside of Joe.

He's coming! The preacher warned,
and you better be ready!
The preacher's words made me think
of my uncle, how sometimes
he would bring me hush presents:
teddy bears, chocolates and a locket–
how I tried to hide when I heard him coming
but he always found me.

Years later, I found trinkets in Liberty's room,
I thought about my uncle–
How no one would believe me
if I told them about what he did.
I wanted to ask her but we just got a new-
used car, a washing machine,
and maybe we do deserve what we get.

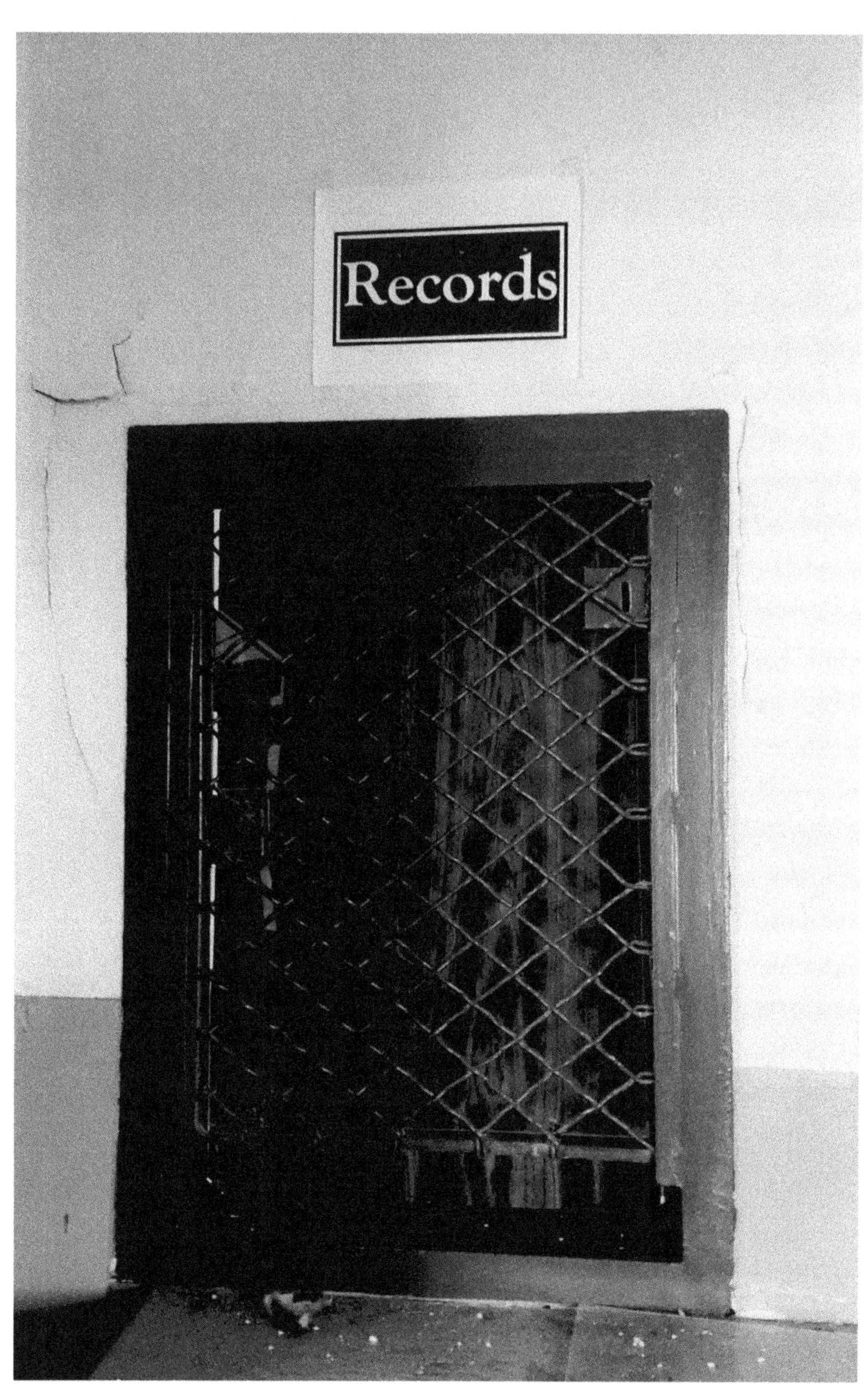
Records

What if

It wasn't
my
fault?

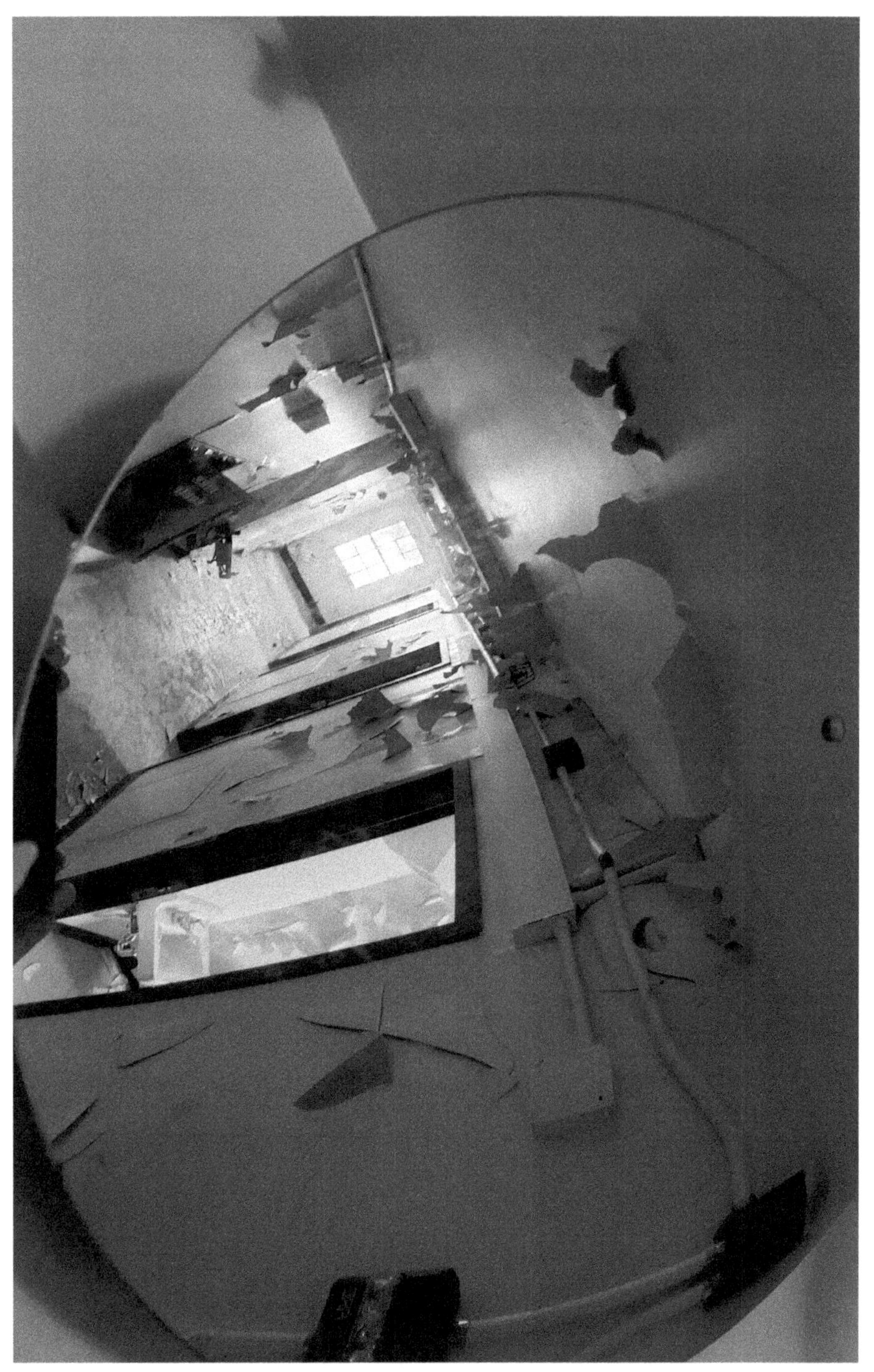

Rearview

From the field near the airport,
from my car, with the doors locked,
I watch Liberty's plane take off.
In my rearview mirror,
the same field
where I was raped
after the homecoming dance
when I was in tenth grade.

Wow, I never said that before–
raped.
I didn't even say it to the Dr.,
my friend's mom brought me to.

I stayed out late,
I had a few beers,
I walked away from my friends,
which made it my fault.

For all those years

I couldn't say
what really happened.

It is easier to lie

motionless,
pretend you are dead
until it is over

and if you find out
it really happened–
that it wasn't just a bad dream
the way I did

you will stalk
the mother of a student,
you will wait for her
in the parking lot of a grocery store.

You will walk up behind her
and ask her
how she could knowingly let
her husband do that to her daughter-
You will tell her she is sick.
When all she can say is Fuck You,
you will push her shopping cart
into her chest.

Then you will drive home-
your own daughter–
the child you kept
because it was your choice
to have her–not one of the boys
in the field that night–
You fell in love and you wanted
to be a mom,
a wife to a man who would never
hurt anyone.
You went the long way around town
to avoid that field.

You never said rape until now.
You could be whoever you wanted to be—
not who some drunk boys in the field
thought you were.

You wait until her plane
is out of sight
and then you unlock and open
your car door fast and put one foot down
on that field because
what they did to you
was not your choice
and you are tired of pretending
that it never happened.

You look up into the sky
and you say—
Rape, they raped me.

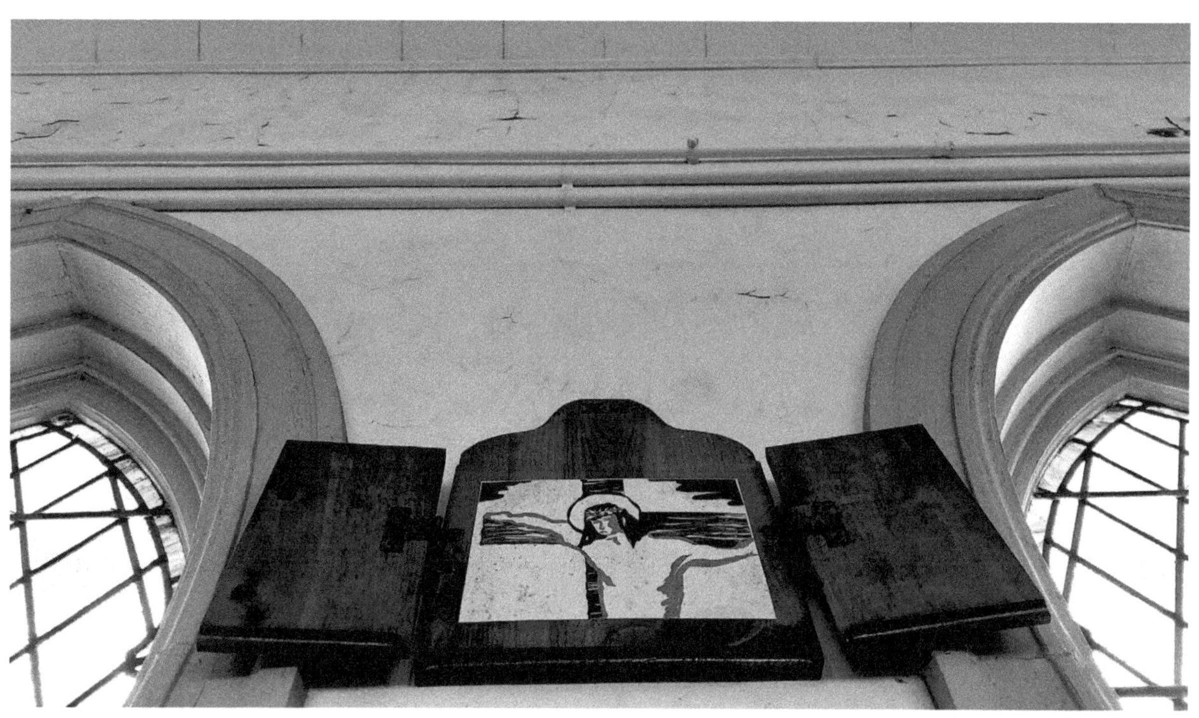

Halo of Stars

When they were done,
the boys in the field
stood above me
arms outstretched
reaching for one another
as if forming a huddle–
I closed my eyes
and I felt a kick, another,
then another.

Come on, let's get out of here,
one yelled.
Dumb slut deserves it!
another answered by stepping on my belly
pushing all the air out of me.

When I opened my eyes,
there was a halo of stars
hoovering in the night sky.
I rolled over, crawled into
a pricker bush and fell asleep.

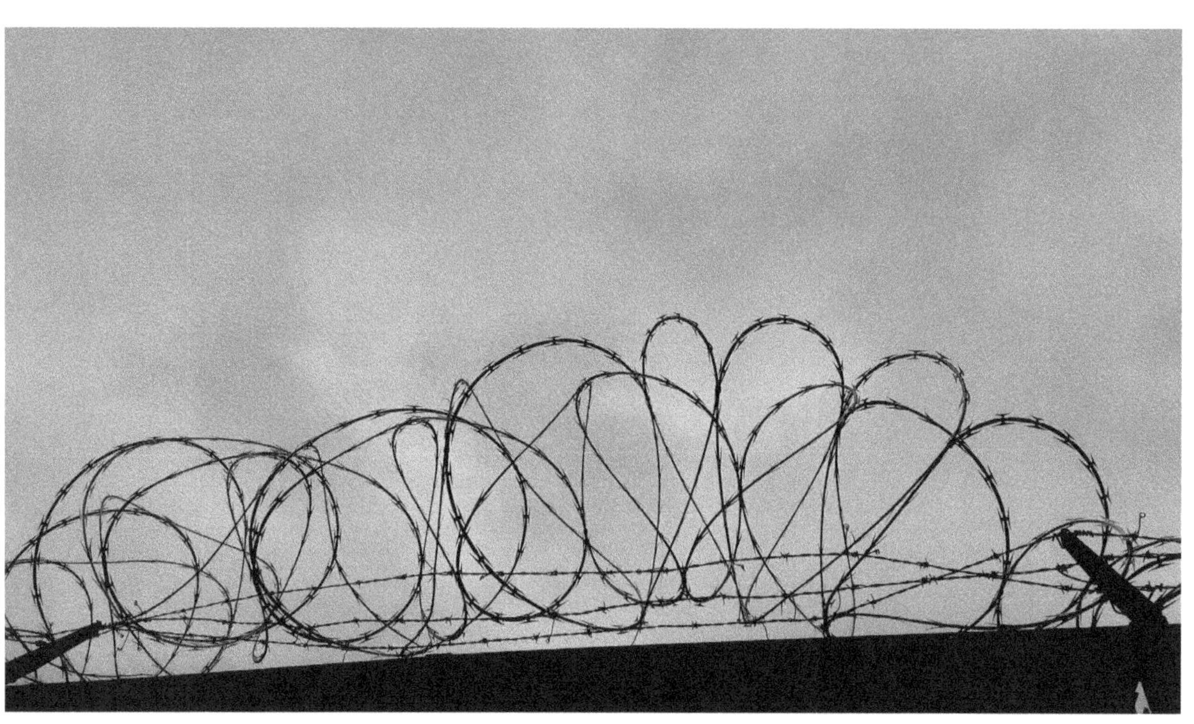

From the Airplane Window

I can see the barbwire on the fence
and I think of my wardens,
of my father writing letters to me,
of my mother telling me I am a lying slut,
of my oldest brother who saw with his own eyes
but still didn't believe,
of the system that lets it happen over and over again
because there isn't enough evidence.

I think of Mrs. Pinsky
how even seven years after having me in class
she still found ways to put gifts in my desks and
lockers. Once she said, *don't you wish you had wings*
and I thought for a minute about the stray cat, about my father,
about *I will find you,*
before shaking my head no.

I think of the boy in the cafeteria,
the one who gave me a pegasus,
the one who never came back the next school year.
I survived because of simple acts of kindness.

The flight attendant
goes over emergency procedures
as I look out the window at the wing of the plane
close my eyes and think about that bluebird,
the one that the cat was batting around,
the one that never had a chance.

Then I remember something as
I listen and shake my head dutifully
to the directions given if suddenly your plane
begins to fall from the sky,
as soon as the cat turned its head,
that bluebird flew away.

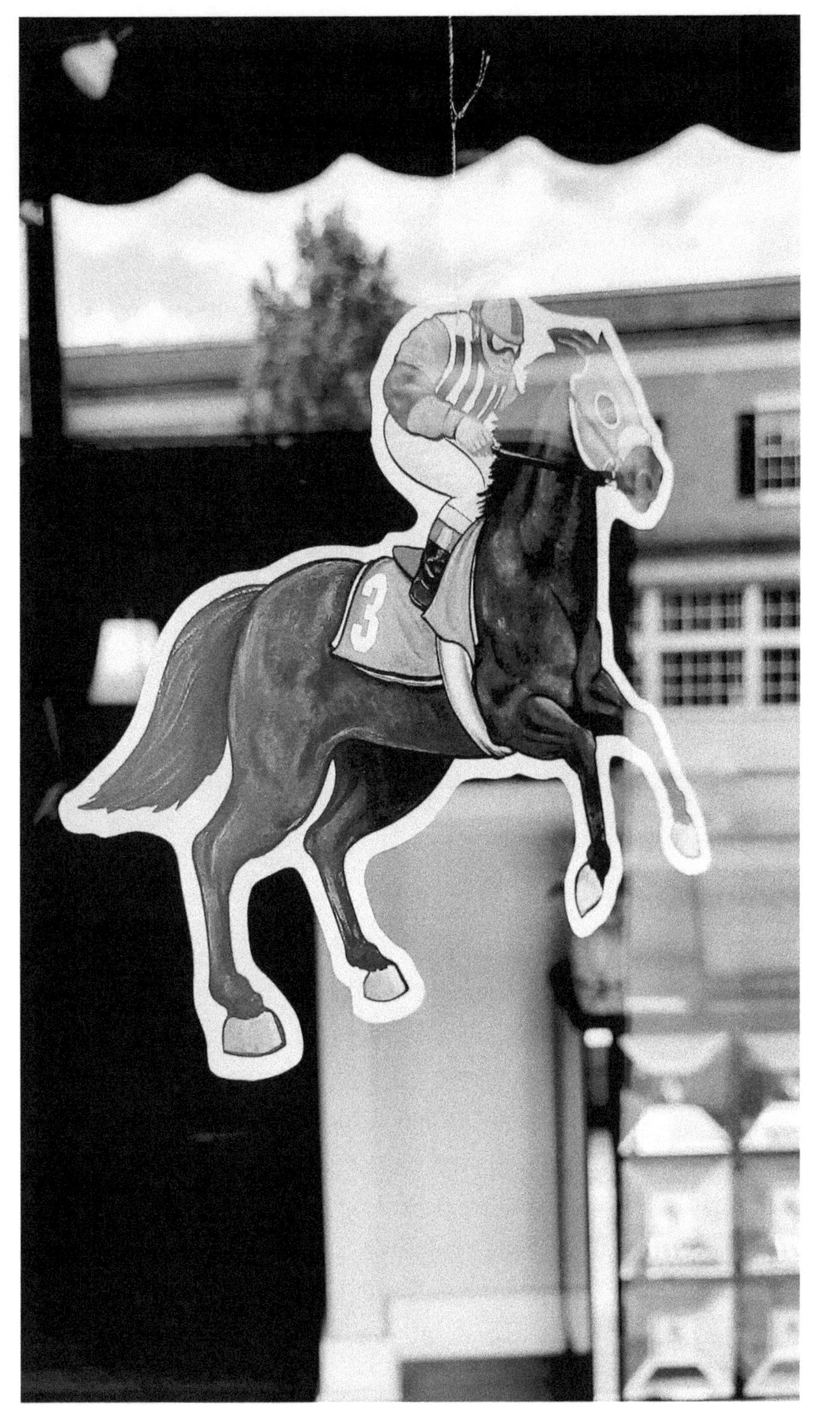

3

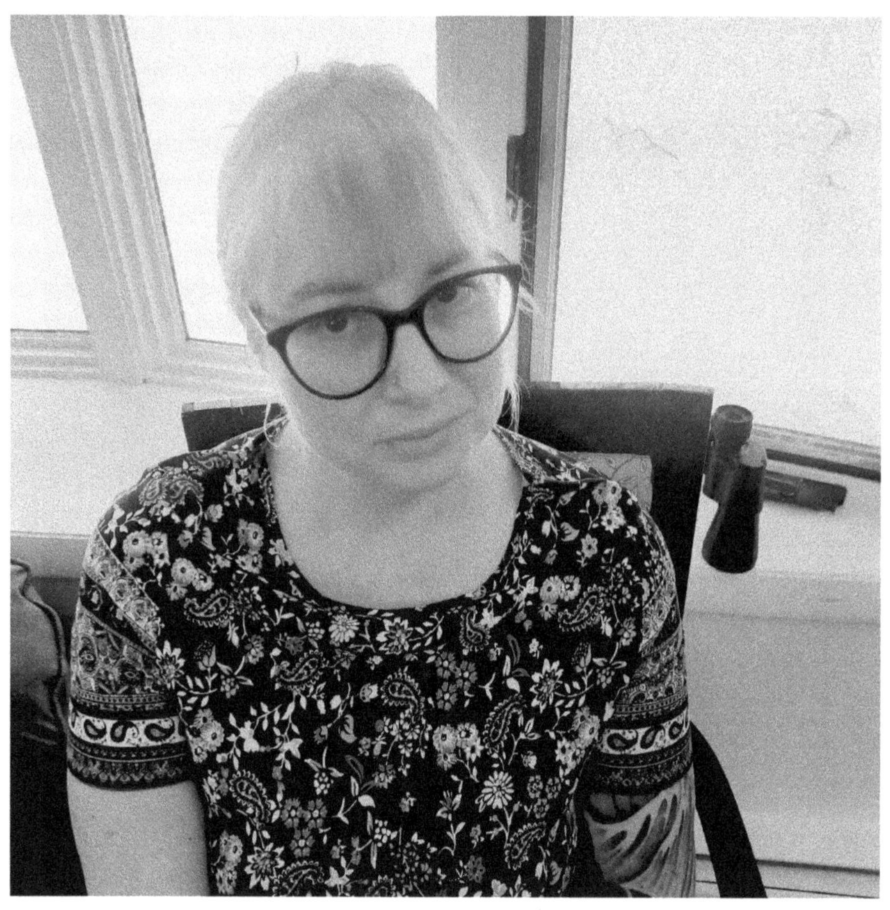

Rebecca Schumejda is the author of several full-length collections including *Falling Forward* (sunnyoutside press), *Cadillac Men* (NYQ Books), *Waiting at the Dead End Diner* (Bottom Dog Press) and most recently *Our One-Way Street* (NYQ Books). Her latest book, *Something Like Forgiveness,* a single epic poem accompanied by collage art by Hosho McCreesh is out from Stubborn Mule Press. Her new collection, *Sentenced,* is forthcoming from NYQ Books. She is the co-editor at *Trailer Park Quarterly.* She received her MA in Poetics from San Francisco State University and her BA from SUNY New Paltz. She lives in New York's Hudson Valley.

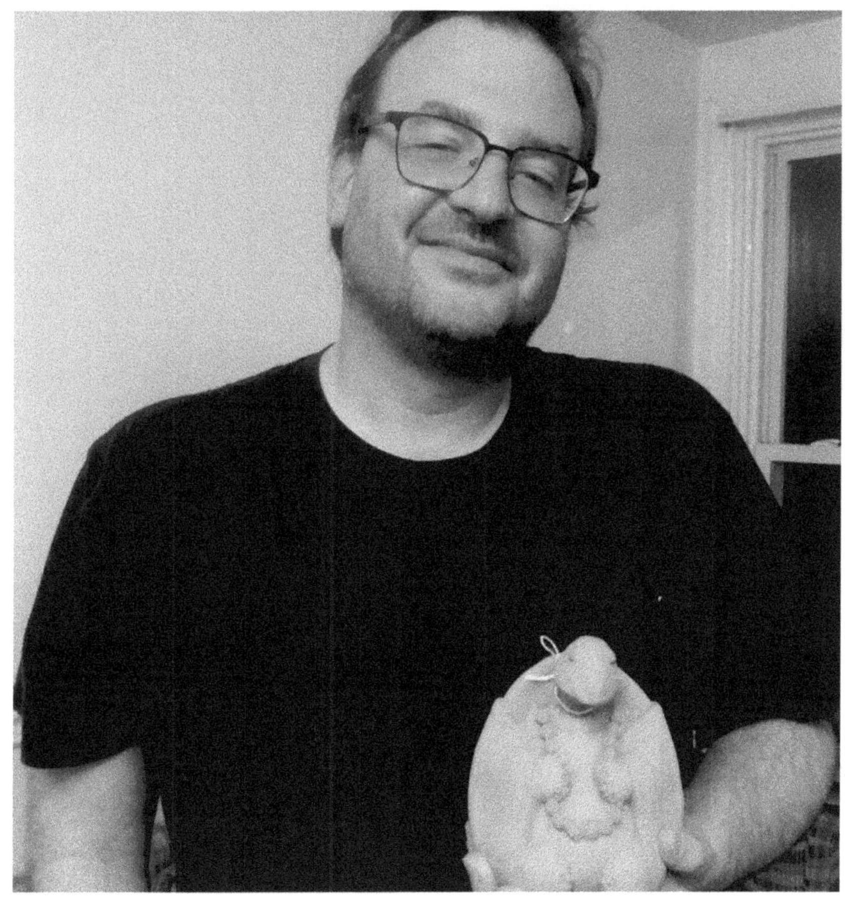

Jason Baldinger was recently told he looks like a cross between a lumberjack and a genie. He's also been told he's not from Pittsburgh but is the physical manifestation of Pittsburgh. Although unsure of either, he does love wandering the country writing poems. He's penned fifteen books of poetry the newest of which include: *The Afterlife is a Hangover* (Stubborn Mule Press) and *A History of Backroads Misplaced: Selected Poems 2010-2020* (Kung Fu Treachery), and *This Still Life* with James Benger. His work has appeared across a wide variety of print journals and online. You can hear him read his work on Bandcamp and on lps by The Gotobeds and Theremonster.

This project was made possible, in part, by generous support from the Osage Arts Community.

Osage Arts Community provides temporary time, space and support for the creation of new artistic works in a retreat format, serving creative people of all kinds — visual artists, composers, poets, fiction and nonfiction writers. Located on a 152-acre farm in an isolated rural mountainside setting in Central Missouri and bordered by ¾ of a mile of the Gasconade River, OAC provides residencies to those working alone, as well as welcoming collaborative teams, offering living space and workspace in a country environment to emerging and mid-career artists. For more information, visit us at www.osageac.org

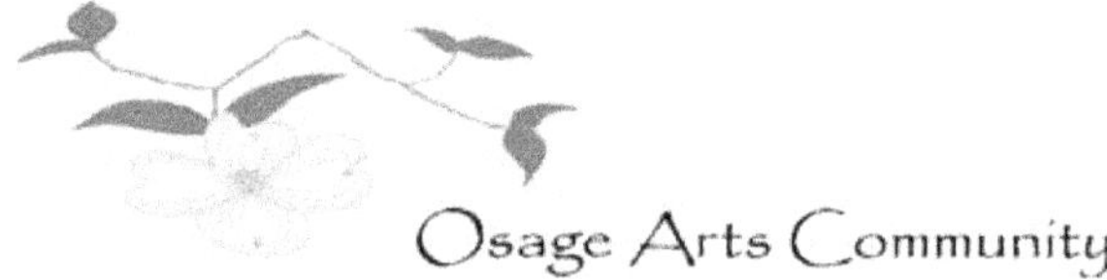